Long Night's Journey Into Day

Long Night's Journey Into Day

The Death March of Lowicz

Erhard Wittek

Heather Clary-Smith / The Scriptorium

8 paws
an army

The Scriptorium

Original German edition: Erhard Wittek: *Der Marsch nach Lowitsch,* Zentralverlag der NSDAP., Franz Eher Nachf. G.m.b.H., Berlin © 1940.

English translation: *Long Night's Journey Into Day. The Death March of Lowicz.* Translated from the German by Heather Clary-Smith under the auspices of The Scriptorium. Copyright by The Scriptorium, Canada ©2015, 2023.
wintersonnenwende.com
versandbuchhandelscriptorium.com

Our cover design shows an excerpt of a map of Poland from 1939. The section outlined in red indicates where the death march of Lowicz took place.

A Note to the Reader: please pardon the occasional incorrect hyphenation at the end of lines. The software with which this book is printed inserts these hyphens automatically, and manual corrections of errors are almost impossible.

Print edition ISBN 978-1-998785-04-9
ebook ISBN 978-1-998785-05-6
First Printing, 2015
Second Printing, 2023

CONTENTS

Map of Poland in September 1939.

Scale 1: 2,000,000

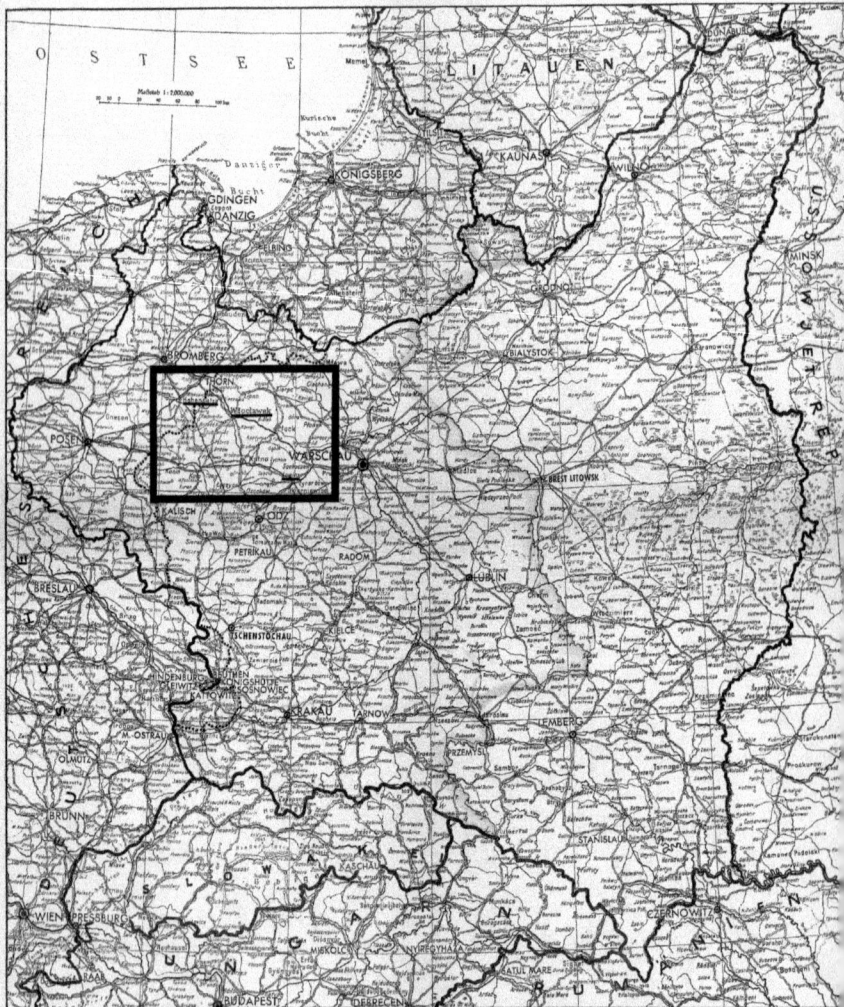

KARTE VON POLEN

Sonderdruck aus dem „Völkischen Beobachter", Münchener Ausgabe, vom 12. September 1939

Einzelverkaufspreis 5 P

Reprint from "Völkischer Beobachter", Munich edition, September 12, 193

The square outline shows the general area of Poland where
the death march to Lowicz took place at the beginning of September 1939.

Please refer to the following page for a more detailed excerpt.

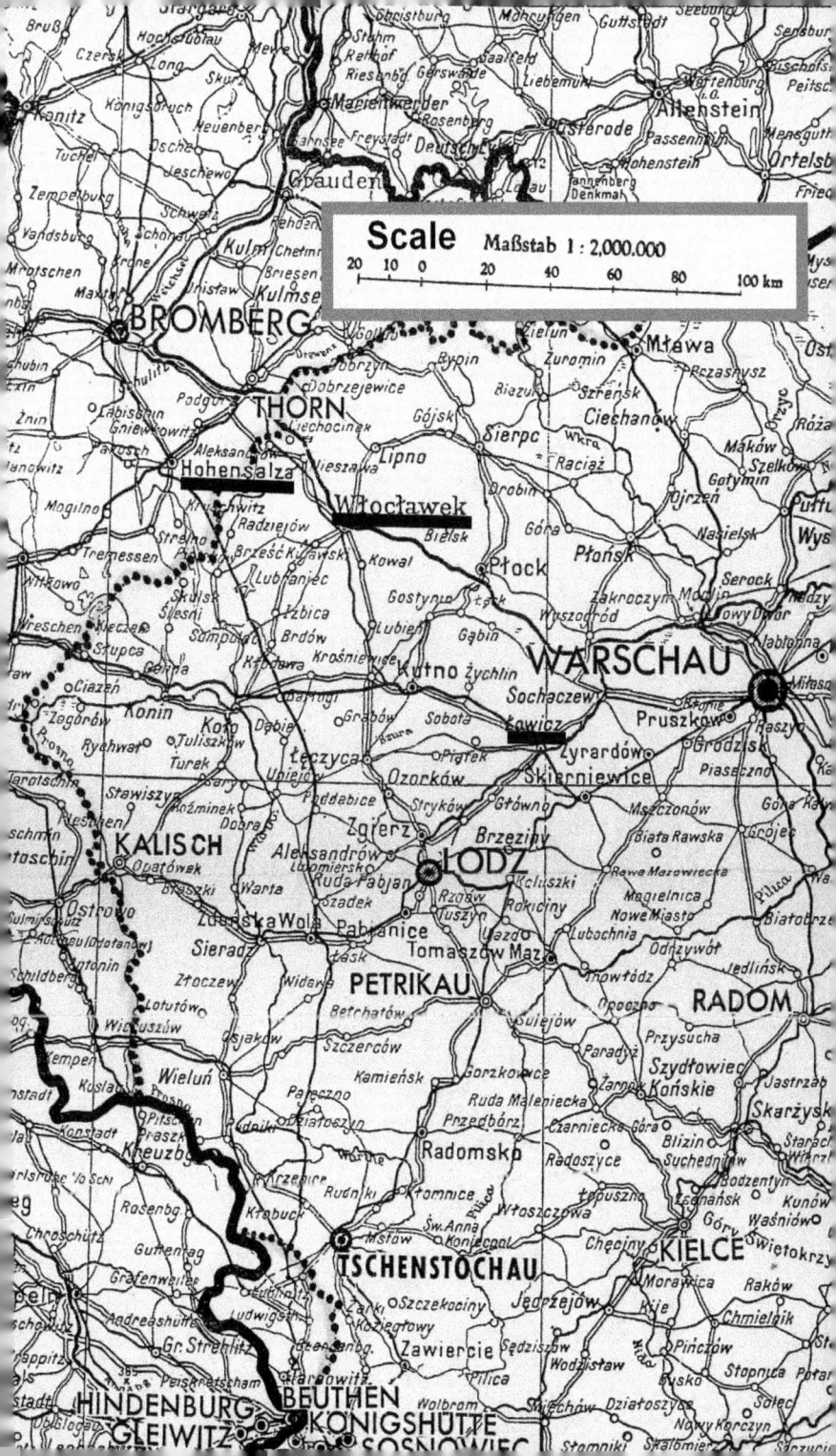

Scale
Maßstab 1 : 2.000.000

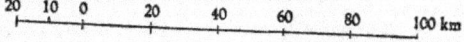

20 10 0   20   40   60   80   100 km

1

The First Few Hours

Reinhold Wittek from Hohensalza in the Wartheland recounts:

When it became clear that the conflict between the Reich and Poland was escalating more and more inevitably towards war, the Germans in my homeland frequently debated whether it would be better to hold out here or to cross the border into Germany. It was obvious to all of us that anyone whom the Poles found in their country after the outbreak of war would have a hard time of it. But the farmers couldn't just leave their land, their farms, their livestock. So it was really only the city dwellers who could have closed up their homes and left to spend a few months in the Reich. The owners of the large estates could have fled as well; they had reliable and loyal German managers to whom they could have entrusted their property. But – if anyone had even really entertained the notion at all – it was clear that it would be impossible to act in such a manner. The Germans in the cities were the leaders of the German ethnic group in political, intellectual and economic respects. They had stated often enough, both publicly and among their friends, that it was important to remain in the country and thus to preserve the Reich's just claim to these large territories that had been stolen from it while it had been powerless, after the war. And when conversations or even thoughts ever got to this point, the matter was decided for the city folk as well.

We witnessed the daily escalation of anti-German incitement in the newspapers and in public gatherings. The process seemed never-ending. Already it was dangerous to speak German on the streets or in public establishments. In 1919 many of the leading Germans here had already had to spend months in the large internment camp Szczypiorno; we knew that as soon as war broke out we would be locked up again; all of us sensed that it would be a harder trial for us this time than it had been in 1919, and those days had truly been hard enough. The hatred harbored by these people, this nation, who had never in their entire history been capable of any truly great achievements in intellectual matters, be they art or science, culture or statesmanship – who rather had spent their entire time of nationhood constantly faced with German superiority in all such matters – the hatred harbored by these people, this nation, grew from the awareness of their inferiority and was fuelled by the realization that some members of the superior foreign nation were now in their power.

We Germans, in so far as we worried about the future, knew this, or at least we sensed it. And our experiences of the last twenty years had trained us to worry about the future, even if one or the other might have been more inclined by nature to let time and events bring what that might. But time and events had already brought everyone enough these past twenty years, and now they were to bring us the **final** test as well.

And even though we knew all this, all conversations in the time prior to the Polish Conflict concluded with the realization that we must remain. Nevertheless, when the danger became ever more immediate there were a few who left the country after all, for what people are completely without weak members!

But for the rest, our attitude was decided by the sense that we were a bastion – soldiers, as it were, of our nation: and the German soldier does not leave his post until he is recalled.

So we got ready. We packed our bags. We hid whatever valuables we may have had, and we got a tough pair of shoes ready for when we might need them. –

On September 1, 1939, shortly before noon, I was arrested in Hohensalza, which the Poles called Inowraclaw. Some Germans in the city had heard the broadcast of the Führer's speech in the Reichstag; the news that war had begun had spread incredibly quickly, as such news tend to do. We felt like soldiers in whose vicinity a heavy grenade with a time fuse had just hit: when will it explode? whom will the shrapnel kill?

I didn't have to wait long. Just before noon, with not a word of greeting, a police officer entered the modest office of the small German bank whose director I was; he had a rifle hanging by its strap over his shoulder, and a revolver in his belt. He was red in the face and sweating, excited and screaming at me, and the sight of the angry Pole quickly helped me to regain my composure. Even though I had fully expected to be arrested: now that the moment had arrived, I admit I had needed to lean slightly against the edge of my desk for a few seconds for support. But the Pole standing in front of me acted as though he were the one about to be dragged off, not his prisoner. Oh yes, this policeman knew very well what they all knew and just wouldn't admit to themselves; he knew what the entire Polish nation knew and what it had sought with its insane chauvinism to cover up against its own sight, namely that any resistance against the German Reich would be futile if ever war actually broke out. That's why this man was screaming the way he was, that's why he was so agitated, that's why he had barged in here with a rifle, revolver and threatening scowls – because he, like all the common folk of this nation, would have felt much safer kissing the seam of the Germans' coats than he felt in his present role.

So I talked to him as calmly as I could and tried not to let him break my composure, and even though my heart was pounding wildly enough, externally I became calmer by the second, and eventually the Pole agreed to accompany me to my home so I could pack a suitcase, since the red warrant he had handed to me stated that I had to come prepared with a change of clothes, a second pair of shoes, underwear, various personal items, and food enough for four days. It all seemed like a standard arrest on proper bureaucratic order. Maybe all our fears had been too pessimistic after all?

There was an uneasy parting at home. My wife stood in the doorway, suppressing tears as she watched me carry my heavy suitcase down the stairs; at the threshold I looked back up at her, tried to smile reassuringly, waved to her with my left hand and called, "So long, Bertele!"

It wasn't far to the police station. The bare rooms of the station already held a few of my acquaintances. We said hello, we shook hands – it was a different handshake than usual; we set our suitcases down and moved closer together, our faces towards the Polish officials, our backs towards the wall or to a fellow German.

As the hours went by the rooms filled up more and more. We stood silently. It was rare that someone whispered a word to his neighbor, it was rare that someone even shifted from one foot to the other. We all knew that this war wouldn't last long; we knew the Polish state too well. Our faith in the power of the Reich and in the Führer's determination knew no bounds. But we also sensed what was in store for us. We were defenseless in the hands of an enemy whose lack of mercy we thought we knew – just as we thought we knew the extent of his hatred. And yet: none of us had an inkling of what was really to come.

Every new arrival was greeted solemnly; every handshake, silently given, strengthened both him and us. Our psychological reserves grew stronger.

Late in the afternoon we were led under heavy guard around the outskirts of the town to the sports field belonging to a Polish club. Here we had to wait outdoors. It was a sunny day, not a cloud in the sky. On the trees the foliage had just begun to take on fall colors. The air was motionless, and it was hot.

The hours went by painfully slowly. At random intervals, more prisoners arrived, individually and in groups. Many of them were being driven in from neighboring towns, on wagons that stopped at the gates of the sports field. From those gates the new arrivals walked over on foot to join the rest of us.

One was a man who had to be carried by four others. He was unconscious. We saw that he was bleeding from his head, face and hands; his other injuries were hidden under his clothes. We found out later that he had been beaten at the city gates by a gang of teenagers with sticks and fence slats until he collapsed. The policeman standing guard over us sent for a medic.

A woman who was clearly just a few months from giving birth came up to us, eyes fixed blankly ahead. She was leading a nine-year-old boy, who walked alongside her hesitantly and silently and stared up at his mother in horror, never looking elsewhere. The woman walked stiffly, did not look to the right or left, staring straight ahead, her movements were lifeless. She joined the other women already waiting on the sports field. They did not pity the newcomer with loud and emotional words as women are normally wont to do; all of them here shared the same suffering and the same fear, and the words that one may otherwise speak so easily and quickly, were inadequate.

It was growing dark. I saw a man sitting on a small wooden crate. He rested his head in his hands and his elbows on his knees; there was something about his posture that made one's heart contract. I learned that the Poles had shot one of his sons, before his very eyes – a son who had protested against his father's arrest and had offered himself to the Poles in his stead. The man's daughter had jumped in to try to avert the disaster – the Poles had stabbed her with their bayonets. Then they had dragged the father away; he had had to leave his daughter lying on the floor where she had fallen with a scream, the way we do not even leave an injured animal behind; the father did not know if she was still alive or if she had died of her injuries.

Darkness fell. Noise and shouting carried over from the town. The sports field was silent. We had joined groups of others we happened to know. There was the seventy-two year old manor owner Stübner from Grossendorf, the farmer Mutschler from Ostwehr, and the young, strong, blond estate owner Meister, there was the aged superintendent Diestelkamp from Hohensalza, the editor Kuss from our German newspaper, there were the manor owners Vollrath Eberlein and Otto Naue – we stood together, sat on our luggage; it was getting colder. Hardly anyone spoke. We resolved to try to stay together through what might come.

About an hour before midnight we were marched off to the train station; guards walked to the right and left of us. Many of us, believing at the time of our arrest that we would be treated properly like prisoners, had packed large suitcases; the walk to the train station was several kilometers long, and not a few almost succumbed to the strain of just this very first march. When we entered the city the streets were relatively deserted, but they quickly filled. It began with loud shouting from individuals and grew within minutes to an inhuman howl from all the windows and doors, side streets and alleys.

The guards pushed back the first ones who tried to attack the marching prisoners, but they did not have the power, nor the will, to prevent the curses and insults that the crowds constantly shouted at us while accompanying our marching rows on either side like packs of slavering dogs. Whenever there was a few seconds' silence, we heard a distant roar that arose in the side streets and quickly neared, we heard the pounding of many feet and the yelling and shouting of those asking about the source of the noise, and of those answering. But then it was all drowned out again in the bedlam of those who had already reached our procession and accompanied us. The city was quite dark, there was no moon, and the first rocks came flying out of the darkness, to be followed immediately by the first cries of pain. As yet there were not many who threw stones or tried to beat the prisoners; it wasn't easy in the darkness to find rocks or cudgels. Also, the guards still tried to hold back the surging crowds, but it was already clear that they were not happy to do so.

For the first time we now heard those words that were to accompany us on our trek through Poland; it was always the same words, and even though we soon became apathetic to all the insults, our sense of honor always reared up again at these accusations: we had always been loyal-to-a-fault citizens of the Polish state!

"Traitors! Spies!" the crowds howled. "They want to send signals to the Germans! What are you marching them off for? Shoot them, give them to us, we'll finish them off, the sons of whores, the Hitler-pigs!"

The insults soon escalated to the point that I cannot repeat them, and more than any other there was always one word that was repeated over and over, which many of us did not know or understand, until one who spoke Polish told us it meant something like "rotting, decomposing dog corpse".

That was our first march through a city. With the exception of those who had been injured, we were still all strong, and we knew how far away the destination of our march, the train station, was. When we finally arrived there, the rabble had to stay back behind the stiles. They were not even allowed in the waiting hall. The platforms were almost empty; cattle cars stood ready, and we boarded them without being harassed further.

Boards were stacked up against one of the end walls of the wagon. The guards ordered us to lay these boards across strong beams running along the side walls. In this way we built a row of benches, where we were told to sit. The policemen took up position at the wagon doors.

As I sat down, someone called to me in happy recognition. I recognized manor owner Lehmann-Nitsche, a man of over sixty, lame on one leg. He too had been deemed a danger to the Polish state and been arrested for it. But as we had seen, even pregnant women were not excepted; in fact, on the sports field I had seen an old hunchbacked woman, half paralyzed on one side and mentally not quite right. She too was a danger to the Polish state, and had been dragged from her home. Lehmann-Nitsche wore only a light linen jacket over his shirt; he had not been given time to dress more warmly. One of our women who had taken an extra coat along had lent him one, which naturally was far too short and tight for him. But it did warm him a little.

Along with Otto Naue, Vollrath Eberlein, old man Stübner and the others, I had been in the first group to leave the sports field. Half an hour later the second group arrived; they had fared much worse than we had. Between our group and theirs, the city had had time to wake up, and the rabble had descended on our comrades with cudgels and rocks, they forced their way onto the train platforms after them, and here, where the group of prisoners separated in order to board the cattle cars, their pursuers escalated to downright madness. They beat the Germans with anything and everything they had. The meager lighting on the platforms shone down on screaming, running figures trying to defend themselves; children sobbed; Polish men and women, out of their minds with hatred and animal rage, beat and kicked, spat and scratched, pounded with bars and sticks against the wagons in which some Germans already sat, and it was probably lucky that the Poles had lost all self-control to the point where they were insane in their raging passions while the Germans gathered together, helped each other, regrouped, and pulled each other into the cattle cars.

Pale and trembling with outrage, I watched the bedlam beyond the open door of our wagon; suddenly I saw the pregnant farmer's wife who had joined us on the sports field that afternoon with her little boy. She ran painfully along the row of cars, pursued by two shrieking Polish women. "Pay attention!" I cried to Otto Naue. "Get ready!" I jumped down onto the platform, pulled the woman closer, suddenly her husband

and boy were there too, we pushed the woman up into our car, two men grabbed her from above and pulled her in, we handed the child up, the farmer, bleeding from head wounds and his mouth, staggered in after, and then they pulled me back up inside as well.

Inside, one of the policemen suddenly stood up. "This is too much," he said, trembling with anger, "this is too much." He gave a few orders, the others jumped up – there were seven guards in the car – took up their weapons, got down onto the platform where a strong band of Poles were just approaching, evidently brought over by the two shrieking Polish women who had beaten the German farmer's wife. Rocks flew in the doorway and crashed against the wooden walls, but then a policeman roared some orders and the doors were closed. Through the small opening that remained, barely a hand's breadth, we heard a wild exchange of words; we heard again the commanding voice of the sergeant, but the masses raged and screamed on.

A short distance away, a dim lamp was lit under the platform ceiling. From the dark of our wagon we could thus see some of what was taking place outside. As always, it was a few ringleaders who distinguished themselves in particular and whom the cheering of the crowd incited to ever more insults. None of them were too insane or offensive, too low, too obscene to be taken up and repeated by the howling mob. And once again the crowd demanded the guards to "give them to us, the Hitler-pigs, we'll slit their guts open, we'll scratch their eyes out, we'll punch their noses in!" What I am recounting here is only the mildest of all the invective.

The rest is unrepeatable. But we heard and understood it all. The mob responded to each such threat with animalistic howls of approval. Someone wrote with white chalk on the outside walls of the wagons: "Twenty hundredweight of pig meat for Warsaw!" and similar epithets, insults of our Führer and our nation – one shrieked with delight as he read the various inscriptions to the others, and more howls of approval followed. All this was accompanied by the thunder of rocks being thrown and bars and sticks being slammed against the wagon walls.

Inside the wagon, we were silent. We sat mute, trying to deal with the nightmare resting on us all. It was like a surreal dream.

Was it over? Was it still continuing?

Suddenly, the little boy's high-pitched voice pierced the oppressive darkness: "Mommy, why are those people so mad at us? It's just because we're Germans, right, mommy?" We heard the nine-year-old speak for the first time, and we remembered that we had seen other children on the sports field too. Some of us suddenly felt tears of anger and helplessness burn in our eyes. The mother answered, in an absent-minded voice, "Yes, my boy, just because we're Germans."

The silence in the wagon seemed to grow even more stifling after these words; but suddenly the farmer's wife began to cry, everyone heard how she sobbed and how a terrible fear shook her. For the men it was almost a relief to hear the woman cry. Her husband tried to console her, hoarsely: "Now, now, Else, hush, it'll pass, they won't abandon us, surely, now don't cry, Else..."

It was clear to us all whom the farmer meant when he said "they". The policemen stood outside the wagon, we were amongst ourselves inside, and old man Stübner said in a clear, firm voice that held no tremor but an unshakeable faith: "No, they won't, Else; no, boy, they won't. They will get us out of this mess, our boys will, and it won't take more than a few days."

The farmer's wife, hearing herself addressed by her first name by a strange man speaking from out of the dark, left off sobbing. It seemed to me that I could feel how she lifted her head in surprise and began to think about the words that had just been spoken. Suddenly, faith stood palpably amongst us in this shabby cattle car in the train station of Hohensalza in Poland. No-one spoke the name, but everyone now thought of him whose voice they had listened to so often with hope and trust as it came to them through the ether. Like a mother, faith stood among us and wrapped her cloak around us all. Suddenly we felt how very much we all belonged together... From that moment on, we all said "du" to each other; formalities were no longer needed or appropriate.

Another voice, also clear and strong, came from a different corner:

"Men, those of you who have something to eat, you must eat now. Eat as much as you can; we don't know if they will take our supplies from us. Those of you who have nothing, speak up, so we can share with you. We will need our strength, so eat!"

We distributed our supplies, which were still plenty, and began to eat. Then we chose a place to spend the night.

Almost all of us had blankets and coats. Things were still bearable.

Finally the policemen got back in, and the train began to move. The raging, howling, shrieking on the platform rose once more to a satanic roar, then it slowly dropped off, the train rolled out of the station, and we were on the open countryside. One of the policemen said that we were headed to Thorn.

The train drove slowly, the rumble of the wheels was soothing, and all of us felt the sudden silence like a blessing. Our overstimulated nerves relaxed, and one after the other we fell asleep.

2

In Thorn and Lipno

We woke up when the train stopped. Daylight shone through the battened hatches of the side walls. We stared at each other, confused; but our gray, bleary-eyed faces showed how memory returned, quickly or more slowly as the case might be for each of us. One man got up and peered through the crack of the door; we were standing in the train station of Thorn, he said, but at the outskirts. The chief of the guards in charge of us permitted the men to step outside to relieve themselves.

They had all climbed back in again when a short, all-but-bald man with a gaunt face, whom I had not met before, suddenly called for silence. I had noticed him several times before due to his calm, composed, self-assured manner. Now the rest of us also heard a droning noise in the air, approaching very quickly; and already, anti-aircraft and machine guns barked and rattled, angry shots rang out from all sides, even the policemen jumped out of the wagons and fired their guns, and we Germans were suddenly alone in the car. The heavy droning was right above us. "Keep calm," I cried. "Don't let them see how happy this makes you!"

There was a howling kind of whistle above our heads, over and over again, then a slamming sound and something bursting nearby, explosions crashed, shrapnel whizzed through the air, the boiling roar repeated and continued, we heard people shrieking horribly, machine guns rattled between it all, the Poles were firing from all sides, ack-ack guns spat and coughed, but already the bomber planes were leaving. The droning faded towards the north, then stopped.

Outside, the policemen stood and yelled over top of each other in confusion. The train began to move again. The guards climbed back in, talking excitedly, each of them telling how he had fired at the enemy and how many he had hit. Suddenly they fell silent. They crowded around the doorway and stared outside. None spoke a word. The train moved along slowly, commanding voices could be heard outside, and between them, moans and whimpers. Over the heads of the Poles I saw the profile of a single brick wall pass by; a shattered window frame hung from it askew; a cloud of brown dust roiled around the reddish-brown rubble.

The train soon stopped again. Twice more, German bomber planes attacked the Thorn train station that day, the Poles grew ever more agitated, but the train bearing our group of prisoners was not hit. We sat in the cattle cars and heard the fists of the German Army pounding into Poland. "Just last night, we were the ones being chased and beaten," was no doubt everyone's thought. "Today, today it's already different."

After a while, quiet returned to the cattle car. The Polish transport leader gathered up his men's dishes and then called Otto Naue and the comrade who had alerted us to the sound of the approaching planes. By now I had found out that he was the farmer Walter Lemke from Luisenfelde. Naue and Lemke spoke fluent and unaccented Polish, and the sergeant ordered them and an auxiliary policeman to fetch tea from the station canteen; but they should take care not to give away that they were Germans. He gave the accompanying guard special instructions to act as inconspicuous as possible, and to leave his rife in the wagon.

Half an hour later they returned with hot tea, cigarettes and a few boxes of biscuits. Naue saw to it that everything was distributed fairly, and we all got enough to drink.

Later, policemen we had not seen before forced their way into the wagon. They were immensely agitated by the air raids, and cursed fiercely at us. One short black-haired individual with a bushy beard and lively, darting eyes was especially hateful. He worked himself up more and more into a wild passion. Finally, he jumped up and tried to throw himself on Vollrath Eberlein who, being blond, stocky and broad in stature, aroused his particular hatred. "That's the right fellow," the policeman screamed, "look at him! He's stuffed himself with Polish sausage and Polish butter, that's how he got so big and strong, chowing down on Polish pork and bacon, and now this vermin wants to wage war on us, because we fed them and didn't let them starve like they have to starve over there with their Adolek, with their little Adolf! Don't look away, you fat Hitler pig, look at me, you'll get your full portion, now you can eat a Polish fist, not Polish sausage!" And he leaped at the man who, rather dumbfounded and a little pale, awaited the attack against which he knew he was not allowed to defend himself. But at that moment the transport leader spoke a few sharp words; the stranger was to mind his own business. If he hated the Germans so much, he should take his gun and go to the front, where he could fight as much as he liked. "But these here are my prisoners, and none of your concern."

The newcomer policemen fell silent, baffled, and the black-haired one was speechless. But then they all began to whisper excitedly to each other. They grew louder and louder, and clearly planned something; from what we could hear, we knew that they were debating whether to send for the station commandant. Clearly a policeman who actually protected his prisoners from maltreatment seemed suspicious to them.

The train's departure thwarted their plans.

Our sergeant, who had kept perfectly calm throughout these discussions, now told us – to the scowls of the strangers – that he was under orders to take us to Wloclawek, but that the direct road there was not clear and so we would have to go via Lipno and Kutno.

It was only the second day of the war, and already one of the country's main traffic arteries was no longer passable. It was obvious to all of us that the phrase, the road was "not clear", was only a poor euphemism for the fact that it had been damaged or destroyed by German bomber planes. We gazed at each other in silence, and our confidence grew. But the strange policemen yelled at us that we had no cause for glee. While the German bomber planes had indeed destroyed the road – our sergeant had not even **hinted** at that! I was just looking at Walter Lemke when they said this, and saw how his clean-shaven, gaunt face came to life – yes, the road was destroyed, but that meant nothing at all, they said. The British navy had bombarded Königsberg, and the city was one big pile of smoking rubble. "Ahl of eet kapuht, house, people, roads kapuht," they added in German and grinned angrily. And in Danzig, they said, a joint British and French army had landed and Danzig was already captured. Polish planes had bombed Berlin. "Ahl of Berlin kapuht, ahl kapuht, ahl of eet!"

Lemke partly closed his left eye and carefully winked at us, but old man Stübner – knowing that none of the Poles would understand him – said in a perfectly calm voice, carrying over the angry chatter of the irate people:

"In your dreams, sweetie!"

It was elegant and sure like the thrust of a foil, timed perfectly to put the opponent out of action with a single move. Julius Mutschler, who sat far away in a distant corner (shrewd as he was, he had put as much distance as he could between himself and the line of fire, just as he always did later; he always made sure that the wagon wall was at his back), Julius Mutschler, who at first had almost fallen for the Poles' tall tales but then, when they became just a bit too tall, had restored his face to the sly little smirk that seemed to always play about his mouth and eyes – Julius Mutschler guffawed loudly, and then broke off in sudden shock.

What did he say?? the short black-haired man, whom the

others called Antek, demanded of old man Stübner. But he looked nonchalantly at the little man, and then looked away again as though he didn't understand him at all. And in fact the Pole grew unsure of himself and seemed not to be certain who had actually spoken at all.

The strangers began to whisper and argue amongst themselves again.

I was sitting none too far from the transport leader, and so I bent forward and began a conversation with him. I had mentally mapped out the route that we were to take now that the direct road to Wloclawek was destroyed, and found the plan so nonsensical that I wanted to try to change it. The route via Kutno was an enormous detour, I told our sergeant.

As we had already seen, he was a man who strove to keep order. But still he felt it was better to be careful. In the course of a long conversation, which I had with him very slowly and with many breaks in between, I tried to bring him around to the idea that it would be better to disembark the train in Lipno and to take a bus or panje cart to drive the 25 kilometers directly to Wloclawek, rather than to take the 200 kilometer detour via Kutno. The sergeant did not say much, mostly just moved his head to indicate doubt, but once he called me *"panie Direktorze"*, Mr. Director. So he must have known who I was; I had never met the man before.

We arrived in Lipno at dusk. The train stopped and the transport leader suddenly ordered that everyone belonging to his group was to get out. So my conversation with him had had some effect after all. We hurriedly gathered our luggage and climbed out of the wagon. It turned out that a total of fourteen of us were in this sergeant's group. Walter Lemke tried to convince him to let the farmer and his wife and son get out as well, but the sergeant refused. He said he had no papers for them. But he instructed an auxiliary policeman to walk with the three of them along the train until they had found the group they were supposed to be part of.

He ordered us to put our luggage down against the wall of the station house and to sit down on it, then posted the guards in a line in front of us. The train began to move again. From the doors, comrades waved to us, surprised to see the small group of us sitting alone on the platform.

The train had stopped only briefly in Lipno, but it had sufficed to draw a sizeable crowd to the station, and they soon began to yell those phrases that all the German prisoners got to hear in those days.

Two half-grown young fellows whom the strange transport had also attracted to the platform had run alongside the train for a short distance, then stopped and ambled back to the station building. They seemed very satisfied with their train-chasing achievement, and when they saw the fourteen of us sitting on our suitcases by the wall like so many chickens on a perch, the no doubt pathetic sight prompted their amusement. They were handsome youngsters, dark-haired and with lively, big dark eyes, slim and tall. Among the Polish leadership elite it is these slender, agile, passionate ones who are the most dangerous, because they see and recognize their people's inferiority on a daily basis, yet their political ambitions and the hot-headed immaturity of their high-flown dreams nonetheless make them wish to rouse their people to great deeds and passions. It is they who have rabble-roused, agitated and incited the fundamentally modest, even humble, hard-working Polish people to that level of megalomania that eventually led to their terrible defeat in this war.

Two young fellows of this sort, therefore, sauntered up to us sitting by the wall, saw the policemen stationed in front of us, and guessed right away who and what we were, and since they were still high on all the nasty, amusing and malicious curse words they had yelled at the "Hitlerowcys" in the train, they were in the mood for more fun. And so they came closer and asked, in German:

"Well, Adolf, are you already here?"

The question was so unexpected that the farmer Julius Mutschler, whose fun-loving nature was ever disposed to laughter, only half-stifled a guffaw and answered:

"Not yet, *panie,* not yet!"

The reply itself was enough to bring about a radical change in the faces of these youths, but it was Mutschler's laugh that aroused senseless rage in a big, broad-shouldered Pole who was just then coming up to us with the usual curses.

The Lipno train station was home to a local chapter of the Polish Red Cross, and the nurses on duty there, who had mistakenly assumed that the arriving transport was one of fleeing Polish refugees from West Prussia, had compounded their error by throwing boxes of cigarettes and biscuits into some of the cattle cars and handing hot tea into the same, for which our comrades, surprised by the unexpected charity, had thanked them gratefully, in Polish of course. When the misunderstanding was cleared up, the Polish nurses promptly forgot their compassion; they broke out into wild curses and insults and felt themselves betrayed, used and laughed at by the Germans; men and half-grown youths joined in, and only the train's departure prevented the first two compartments, which had received the most charitable gifts, from being stormed.

Now the crowd was returning, with a single, huge Pole in laborer's clothing far in advance of the rest. He had overheard Julius Mutschler's laugh; now we heard one of the two youths translate Mutschler's answer for him. He bellowed and charged our startled comrade like a bull, head ducked down and huge hands bunched into fists. "You pig want to laugh, you stinking cadaver, you laugh!" he raged, but two of the guards barred his way with their rifles and forced him back.

By now, news of the arrival of an entire train filled with the hated Germans had evidently spread through the city, and ever more crowds of Poles came rushing to the station. At first they seemed to want little more than to see what was happening. Between two and three hundred people gathered in the small station square within just a few minutes. The raging Pole turned to them. "They are protecting him! We're not supposed to touch them, the choleras, the Hitler swine, the traitors, spies, sons of whores!" His words tumbled over each other, and the big, heavy, hulking fellow spat, spewed, raged the curses out rapid-fire without ever being at a second's loss for more.

The surrounding crowd was seized by a crazed fury, raging hatred, mass insanity – call it what you will, they were seized by the devil. Men roared and screamed, they ran around like rabid dogs, searching for a cudgel, a rock, an iron bar, women shrieked and howled, their faces contorted into horrendous grimaces that had nothing human left in them – with horror we even saw that many of these creatures were foaming at the mouth, that's how much their blind rage, their hatred born of fear, their blind passions had overcome them. We were unable to remain sitting on our luggage, we stood up and leaned against the wall – we did not look at each other for we could not look aside. Like a bird transfixed by the sight of the snake we had to keep staring into the raging, roaring mob before us, but I think we all felt that our faces were as white as chalk.

Our transport leader had left for a few minutes to try to arrange for a bus to drive us to Wloclawek. He returned at the very last second. He pushed through the crowd that parted for him very reluctantly; the policemen, who may have felt that they themselves were in danger as well, had taken up their rifles, and that alone had dammed the flood of insane hatred a little. The sergeant was pale right to his lips. In a piercing voice he shouted an order in Polish, and the guards snapped their rifles high and released the safeties.

There was sudden silence. The sergeant, so enraged that he stuttered a little, shouted that anyone harming his prisoners would be shot. Everyone was to leave the platform immediately.

It was strange to see baffled amazement spreading over the rage-contorted, teeth-gnashing faces. A few Jews who had raged and incited in the background were the first to depart. Some women, on hearing the word "shot", shrieked and ran away. Some comparatively docile individuals, who may have been ashamed of their loss of control, followed; others who had been more in the role of curious onlookers – yes, there had been some of these as well – protested and cursed but vanished as ordered, and suddenly our sergeant was left with a remainder of thirty, forty, fifty or so men who looked, embarrassed and uncertain, to the left and right and everywhere except at him, and who clearly, being faced with the police, suddenly remembered any number of things they might have done, to which they would not want to draw the attention of the authorities. They were not the kind of persons who care to have anything to do with a policeman. And when the sergeant, who had recovered his composure, now asked them sharply what they were doing here, and why they had not yet reported to the military, seeing as it was war?, they too trundled off, muttering and scolding softly to themselves.

We sat down on our luggage again; no wonder that our knees were trembling. We had just been preserved from unspeakable maltreatment – in fact, I believe we had just avoided death. We spent several more hours waiting in this train station, and were subjected to curses and insults several more times. "Hitler swine" was the least we were called, but things did not escalate to any real danger again.

Once darkness had fallen, the sergeant led us through the town to a large building, in front of which we again had to wait for a long time. Then some panje carts pulled up. Our transport leader had somehow managed to procure them. We got on them, the policemen followed suit, and the drive southward began.

The carts shook and rattled, their wheels grinding through

the sand on the road, the horses snorted, every now and then one of the coachmen called out something in Polish, and the policemen, two of whom were on each cart, talked amongst themselves; we were silent. Outside, there was war. The wide, flat land lay calm and quiet, it replied with silence to all the unspoken questions roiling within us. From the east, the wind came softly across the fields as it had always done, and the stars twinkled above in a clear sky.

The night grew bitterly cold. Later, the moon rose – a narrow red sickle. Every now and then, to one or the other side of the road, a village emerged from the uncertain darkness. The small straw-covered huts swam singly like boats at anchor in the fog covering the fields, under shivering poplar stands.

Later we came through some woods where advancing troops crossed our path. The soldiers learned from our guards who we were; immediately, the same old curses and insults began here as well, we were threatened and treated to the usual descriptors. But since our carts kept moving and the troops were forbidden to stop, nothing more came of this, until suddenly a mounted officer rode up to our cart and roared at us from horseback, waving his revolver around as though he wanted to shoot.

Old man Stübner, whose white hair shone in the darkness, said in his aged but still powerful voice: "I was a German officer. Shoot, why don't you! But don't think for a second that we are afraid of you." His clear, firm words baffled the Pole, who lowered his weapon and stopped his horse. Our cart drove on. Soon the Pole vanished in the darkness.

Hours later we saw the Vistula, broad and white. Our carts

drove down from the higher ground into the valley, the countryside drowning in fog; the carts rumbled across the bridge, and anyone who had been asleep awoke. The carts shook and rattled us across the uneven city streets and stopped outside a big lowering building.

The transport leader got down and knocked on the iron gate of a huge, darkly lurking entranceway, he had to pound repeatedly against the resonating metal and finally resorted to the butt of his rifle. His powerful blows echoed dully from the walls. Finally there was a sound of approaching footsteps, a small square hatch at eye level was lifted, a pale ray of light fell onto the street, then the gate opened its maw.

Stiff and over-tired, we climbed down from the carts, carried our suitcases into the entrance and lined up in rows of two without anyone telling us to do so. It was better to do it ourselves than to have to obey the Poles' orders.

The sergeant spoke with a prison official, handed him a sheaf of papers, a roll-call was taken, all of us were present and accounted for. Finally the transport leader turned to us again. We saw his pale, thin face in the glow of a dim electrical bulb dangling from the arch of the doorway, swinging slightly in the breeze.

The Pole's face was solemn and reserved. He said, he had brought us to the prison of Wloclawek in accordance with his orders. His job was thus done. He paused; it seemed as though he wanted to add something, but then he turned away with a curt *"Dobra noc!"* – Good night!

The heavy iron gate swung open, then closed behind him. Each of us would have liked to shake his hand. He had done his duty, properly as should have been a matter of course. But we knew this country, and we knew that in Poland it is not a matter of course to act as this man had acted.

3

In Wloclawek Prison

A man in a greenish-gray uniform, with a squashed face sporting an excessively large crooked nose, led us into the building while two uniformed guards brought up the rear. We had to line up in a bare, dirty hallway and then were called by twos into a room where two men sat behind a wooden divider. We had to identify ourselves and to hand over all our valuables and luggage as well as our jackets, suspenders, belts and pocket knives. I also had to give up my glasses, and from that moment on I could only get around with hands outstretched before me, as I am very nearsighted. Then the short man with the crooked face took charge of us again, leading the way bow-legged, flat-footed and dragging his feet. The fellow was a Jew such as is commonly depicted in caricatures, but his face did not look quite as low-class as the rest of his stature seemed.

He took us to the second story, into a large empty prison cell six double steps long and perhaps four wide. In the time that followed we had more than enough opportunity to walk its measure in both length and breadth. The room had a cement floor; up against one wall there leaned a wooden board, two trestles that might have served as table legs, and a bench. Also, at about head-level, a board was affixed to one of the side walls, with a sort of dowel running underneath.

I was one of the first to enter this cell; the others followed one by one. They looked around the large, electrically lit room in obvious befuddlement. The ride on the jerky, rattling carts that magnified every pothole and rock in the road into hard jolts had been torture in the end; it had been especially hard on the older men. Herr Heinecke from Wybranowo, more than sixty-five years old and with a severe heart condition, had so far taken all the strain and hardships with something akin to humor, but now he dropped onto the bench and put his hand over his heart with a tired, almost absent-minded gesture. We moved the bench closer to the wall so he could lean against it. The Jew – by now we had found out that he was the guard of this part of the prison – had processed the old gentleman last. The endless standing and waiting in the bare hallway had cost him the last of his strength; but the guard had forbidden him to sit even though he saw that he was staggering from weakness.

Exhaustion overcame us all. For a few hours at least, we hoped, we would be safe. We stretched out on the concrete floor and tried to sleep. But barely half an hour passed before there was a banging on the door, rough voices could be heard, a key grated in the lock, and the guard came in. Two uniformed men loomed behind him. The guard looked searchingly through the room on whose floor the prisoners were sitting up, some of them sleepy, some startled, some groaning in pain for the cement floor was hard on all our bones. The guard gestured to Julius Mutschler, yelled at two others to get up and follow him, and after he left the cell with our three comrades the door crashed shut again.

It had been a strange interlude, and the Jew had grinned so nastily. Those of us left behind gazed at each other silently, no-one spoke what everyone thought but we all realized that we shared the same ominous suspicions. A stocky man, manager of a large co-operative, who had been a bit of a braggart and also not always a very pleasant person in other ways before the war – how long ago that seemed, how endlessly long ago that it had been peacetime! and yet today was only the third of September! – this man, therefore, now whispered in horror: "They won't shoot them, will they?" Suddenly he lost his composure (he had demonstrated rather weak nerves before this incident too) and shrieked, "for God's sake, they're not going to shoot us, are they?!"

Angrily, Walter Lemke said, "shut up, Rehse. The Poles don't shoot anyone just like that." But he spoke hoarsely, and his face too was pale. "One time I spent four months in Wronke prison, I know how these things go. They're probably going to interrogate us, or something like that."

What else could we do but believe what Lemke said. But now another faint-of-heart began to lament: "Oh if only I had been different towards the Poles, if only I had learned to speak Polish! What good is being German to us now..."

At that, Lemke, who had been sitting on the floor with

his back against the wall, jumped up with surprising agility. The normally so calm, rather slight man was as though transformed; he marched up to the complainer and said, in a voice like ice, he should be silent, for he, Lemke from Luisenfelde, would tolerate not one word of cowardice. He had balled his hands into fists and it was clear to see that he would rather have used them than listen to such weakling complaints.

We stretched our aching joints out again on the cement floor and tried to sleep. But none of us managed. What were they doing to Mutschler? And why him in particular? And Stübner and Kepler? Why those three, specifically? We recalled what we had seen and heard in Hohensalza on the sports field, we remembered the raging mob in Lipno – was that really only twelve hours ago?

There was more banging at the door, the Jew reappeared. This time he'd even brought a woman along. She peered over his shoulder, puffy-eyed. The guard again yelled at two of us to get up, waved them rudely over to him: "Out with you!" he said. The woman prodded him – now we saw that she too was wearing some kind of uniform – she prodded the guard and pointed to Rehse, who sat pale and panting, staring with horror at the two people who wielded such power over others here. The Jew laughed. "You too!" he yelled, "up, come, quickly!" Rehse shuddered back, but then he pulled himself together, got up, and obeyed silently.

"Lemke, what does all this mean?" old man Heinecke asked.

"How would I know?" the tough little man replied. "I think they just want to wear us down. All of you, be quiet and don't let them see you're worried."

The next time around, the Tschekist – as we had already begun to call the guard – fetched Lemke, old man Heinecke, and me. Outside the door stood two men in uniform, but we saw that they were neither policemen nor soldiers, but wore the same badges as the guard. So they were prison officials. They also had no guns.

We were taken two stories down to the ground floor, through long hallways and down echoing stone stairs. The morning sun shone in, and light and shadows danced on the floor underneath a window outside of which we could see a tree in radiant yellow foliage. A cell was unlocked for us. We entered and – stood face to face with Stübner, Mutschler and Kepler. "What's going on?" asked Julius Mutschler. "What's happening? What are they doing to us?"

"There you are!" the three of us replied, heaving a sigh of relief.

"They brought us here, and then they left us standing. Look at that on the floor – over there!" said Mutschler darkly. His sly smile was completely wiped from his face.

A small iron ring was set in the middle of the floor. Aside from it, the cell, which was much smaller than that in the second floor, was completely empty. The six of us stared at the small ring, so harmless-looking. What did it mean? Is that where they tied their victim when they...? Probably none of us finished the thought. As yet our imagination fought against the thoughts of what fate might be in store for each of us. A ring like that – its only purpose could be to tie something to it. What could one tie to it in a cell that holds nothing, absolutely nothing other than six prisoners?

The morning sun shone in through a small window. The bars cast their patterned shadow on the floor.

Half an hour later they brought Rehse in. He entered, looked around fearfully, saw us sitting on the floor or walking up and down the cell, and could not believe his eyes. "What, what's happening..." he stuttered.

They had taken him to a cell by himself, and left him sitting there alone.

"Didn't I tell you? They're trying to wear us down. It's fine, now we know!" cried Walter Lemke. His voice was no longer hoarse as before, it had its old bright tone again. "Here, smoke, I have some cigarettes left." He took a box of matches. "Watch, you can learn to do this." He took his knife and split the thin match lengthwise into four sections. "I learned that in Wronke. I was imprisoned once before, for political misdemeanors. I think our stay here won't last four months like mine did that time." He started on a cigarette, passed it on, it made the round among us, everyone took a drag and no-one thought it strange to smoke a cigarette that someone else had already had in their mouth. We all sat down on the floor, leaned against the walls, tried to sleep, and greeted, with low voices but shining eyes, everyone who was brought in next. Some two hours later we were all together again in this new cell.

But hardly had we all settled down, crowded closely together, before the door opened again and a guard appeared. This time it wasn't the Jew. But what a face this fellow had! He held his head bent far forward, grinning stupidly and maliciously, peered at each of us in turn as though he were choosing a victim, relishing the doubt in all those pairs of eyes which reflected uncertainty again, and then he gestured to me. "You, over there, come!" But without my glasses I could not tell that he meant me. Also, we were sitting so closely together that Walter Lemke, who sat beside me, thought the fellow meant him, and started to get up. "No, dammit, the other one, beside you!" the guard shrieked. "Move, buddy, or do I have to help you?"

I got up, the door slammed into its lock behind me, the key rattled as it turned. And then I saw, before me in the middle of the hallway, a chair, and beside the chair a man in prison clothes, holding some kind of shiny object. Even though it was only a few meters away it was all blurry to me, all I could see was the glint of sunlight on steel or nickle but I thought, well, they probably won't cut my throat right here in the hall-way. I was made to sit down on the chair, the man in prison clothes lifted a tool and – shaved my head bald. I already felt almost like a real prison inmate; and what must my comrades imagine was being done to me, after I had been singled out like I had!

When the man was finished, a different inmate took me to a supply room where I was given a striped shirt, a blanket, towel, spoon and bowl, for which I had to sign in a big book. Then I was taken back to the large cell in the second story where we had all been before. In one corner of the room lay a pile of straw sacks. I counted them. There were more than thirty. So everyone would get one. It seemed we had been deemed worthy of some basic creature comforts.

In the course of the next few hours one comrade after the

other reappeared in this cell until we were all reunited without exception. Then the guards even brought us our food which had been confiscated on our arrival, and at the same time we got a new cellmate, a Pole, who entered with a bucket of drinking water. The newcomer, a short, lively, energetic man with a sly cast to his eyes, was introduced to us as our overseer, who would ensure order and whom we were all to obey. "Aha, the Cell Senior!" said Walter Lemke, who was already familiar with how things were in Polish prisons.

While we ate and drank, the Pole inquired about the various inmates. He had sat down on the bench beside me, pointed first at one, then at another, demanded to know their names and civilian professions. "Oooh, a manor owner?" The Pole opened his eyes wide. "So, how much does he own? I mean, how many morgen of land?" "Well, probably about five or six thousand." "And that young one, is that his son?" "No, that's a landowner too, he owns 960 morgen." And so he asked on and on, and his astonishment grew.

"So, so; they're all noble gents, big men. Well, whenever I get out of here, and I come to see you all, you'll help me, won't you, hmmm?"

"That depends," I replied, cautiously and in the same clumsy way the Pole himself spoke. "If you, you know, if you're not mean to us... But what's your story?"

"Oh, me, I have nothing. My father has four morgen land, I work for him."

"But why are you here in prison?"

"Ah, well, was a dance in the village, were other fellows

there too, we played around a bit with knives, someone died. Ah, well, someone had to go to prison, they picked me."

Suddenly he lifted his head and called angrily: "What are you doing? Can't you drink properly, do you have to spill? Take a rag, right now, wipe it up! It'll leave spots, and the *pan przodownik** will be mad!" (*The prison warden: "Mr. Warden".)

Old man Heinecke was the culprit; he had spilled a few drops of water while scooping with his cup from the bucket. Young Meister took a rag. "Don't worry, I'll take care of it!" he said and rubbed the floor until no damp was left. Panje Killer, who had "played around a bit with knives", inspected the floor to make sure it was dry again.

Then he stood by the door and said, what counted was to earn the *pan przodownik's* good will. Everything had to be neat, cleanly swept, no dirt on the floor, no spots, nothing. When Mr. Warden came we would all have to line up in rows of two and greet him, and when he left we also had to greet him. And he would practice it with us. Then he roared: "Attention!"

He lined us up in order of size and said, this was how we would always have to stand as soon as we noticed the door being unlocked. And the greeting was, *"Dzien dobry, panie przodowniku!"** He would practice that with us too. "Attention!" he yelled. And we all said, *"Dzien dobry, panie przodowniku."* (*"Good day, Mr. Warden!")

That was children's blabber, not a greeting of men, said Mr. Killer, "louder!"

"Dzien dobry, panie przodowniku!" we yelled.

Yes, he said, that was better, but one of us said it slowly, the other fast. We should watch his hand, he'd give us the beat.

"Dzien dobry, panie przodowniku!" we now roared, in unison.

Good, he said, but we needed to practice. Again!

"Dzien dobry, panie przodowniku!"

Again! And again! And... no, not loud enough. Again!

"Dzien dobry, panie przodowniku!"

Yes, now we were all laughing. That didn't bother him, said our dear Mr. Killer, but when Mr. Przodownik arrived, none of us must laugh or even twitch our lips. Mr. Przodownik had no sense of humor. So, one more time, all of us together now:

"Dzien dobry, panie przodowniku!"

And so we repeated the greeting over and over again, at the top of our lungs, until suddenly the key was heard turning in the lock. The Pole raised his finger, we squared our shoulders – after all, almost all of us had been German soldiers at one time – the door opened, and in came a guard with a prisoner carrying a steaming bucket of food. The greeting was unnecessary. "Eight portions," said the guard, "for those with the red warrants. The others provide their own rations." The eight stepped forward, held out their bowls, the inmate put one scoop into each bowl, but the guard – the first person we had seen so far among all the personnel who had a decent face – said that he should fill the bowls all the way. And in this way each of us got a bit of warm soup, for just as we had shared our provisions in the morning, the eight soup recipients now shared with everyone.

"Aha!" said Walter Lemke, "it's the first Sunday of the

month today, that's stew day." Our mood had mellowed during the meal, even though the broth in the bowls looked rather suspect. We tried not to think about what the state of cleanliness in the prison kitchen must be. But it was a warm meal, the first warm meal for all of us since September the first. And today was already the third day of our imprisonment, the fourth or even the fifth for some others.

"Eat up!" said Lemke, "leave nothing over. We'll need our strength."

Some time after the meal the door was unlocked again. "Twelve men!" yelled the guard. And our Killer added in explanation, "Anyone who has to go badly, go first!" (He put it rather more bluntly.) In the corner behind the pile of straw sacks stood a bucket with a tight-fitting lid, but it was only to be used in emergencies, as Killer Senior had warned.

We were ordered to bring our towels and food bowls along. The wash room had twelve taps and we all washed up with abandon and downright delight; it was the first time since our arrest. The food bowls also had to be cleaned on this occasion. But each group was given a mere ten minutes.

"*Psia krew!*"* Walter Lemke said respectfully when he returned, "such strict *porzadek.*** This place is a real luxury hotel." It soon became apparent in this prison that Lemke, a slight, short man, a farmer from near Hohensalza but with small, slender hands like a woman's, had a calm fearless nature and almost serene composure that made him equal to anything. (*Polish curse; literally, dog's blood. **Order.)

Time passed. Some began to tell stories of what they had experienced, and soon the room resounded with jokes both good and bad. But none of us dared mention the war and how it might be going; we did not trust the Pole. Who knew if maybe he understood German after all.

But the Pole in question suddenly began to scold loudly: what a mess, he said. Hadn't our mothers taught us neatness? "Look at how the towels are flung across the bar! Just like that! No, no!" And he showed us how it should be done. He folded a towel lengthwise by a third, took it in his hands by either end and drew it back and forth across the table's edge a few times until it got a sharp crease, as though ironed. Then he folded the other long edge over as well, so that the entire towel now had only a third of its original width, and drew it over the table edge a few more times. Then he folded it in half and hung it over the wooden dowel that ran along the wall under the shelf. And everyone should remember which spot was theirs! (He had taken the first spot, of course.)

We had watched our teacher closely and now stood around the table busily ironing our towels. Then Walter Lemke arranged them dead straight on the dowel, making sure that none hung lower than any of the others. We were quite pleased with our work, another fifteen minutes had passed, and we had to admit to our Killer Cell Senior that yes, it looked much better now.

In the afternoon I happened to be standing by the door, scooping some water from the bucket that stood right by the entrance, when the door opened and another inmate entered the cell. There was a general Ah! of greeting.

"Here, take!" I said to him in German and held the water

scoop out to him, for I knew that they were all thirsty and of course I believed the newcomer was a German too.

But he said proudly, *"Od niemcza wode nie biere!"* I don't take water from a German.

Whoa, I thought, here's one who is better than we are. And I was right. He later introduced himself to our Killer Senior as a vice-Starost, in other words, a government official.

"Well, what do you think he did," the Cell Senior said when I asked him later. "He got caught. You know there are two kinds of officials in Poland, those who got caught and those who will. Well, he's the first kind. He probably helped himself to a bit from the cash box, a bit too much I'd guess, since they don't care about small amounts in our administration."

There were other such characters among us in this prison. For example the inmate who had recorded our personal data the day we'd arrived had been First Secretary at the Wloclawek District Court!

Afternoon passed, it grew dark. The warden stopped at our cell on his evening rounds, we heard the key turn in the lock in time, lined up, and shouted our greeting:

"Dzien dobry, panie przodowniku!"

He grinned maliciously and asked our Killer if anything new had happened; the government official had to report. "Ah, a vice-Starost!" said the *przodownik.* "A fine gentleman. We have other fine gentlemen here. Helped yourself to a bit from the till, hmm?" The starost replied with a noncommittal shrug; clearly he would have liked to deny it because we were there, but didn't really dare do so since the *przodownik* knew the reason for his arrest perfectly well. When he left we roared after him:

"Dobra noc, panie przodowniku!" ("Good night, Mr. Warden!")

The fellow really did nothing worth mentioning to us while we were at that prison. But his furtive gait, the gloating look on his face, his eyes that never looked straight into ours – all that made him less than popular with us.

We put the straw sacks on the floor one beside the other and lay down to sleep. But our Cell Senior called two of us over to help him reassemble the table in a corner of the room so that it stood lengthwise along the wall, and then he nonchalantly selected the best-stuffed straw sack and displaced the comrade already sitting on it – I think it was Rehse. Rehse had to get himself another one from the pile, while our Killer Senior placed his on top of the table. That's where he slept, three feet off the floor and higher than the common folk. But before he retired to his perch he did five minutes' gymnastics. He stood with his back to the wall, gathered his strength for a moment and then started on a high-speed march through the cell. Staring fixedly at the floor before him, he walked with small, fast, firm steps to the opposite wall, turned quickly around, walked back, turned again, and repeated the maneuver some twenty times more. We watched him with a fair bit of astonishment. When he felt he had done enough, he went to his bed, took off his shoes, laid down on his straw sack, covered up with his prison-issued woolen blanket, and was sound asleep just a few short minutes later.

We had watched in baffled amusement. Lemke, whose

straw sack was on the floor next to mine, now said softly: "Well, he needs it. He's got six years left to go. For us it probably won't be more than another six days." And with that, he too stretched out. "Like I said, a downright luxury hotel," he added with an almost hedonistic growl. "There's even a blanket! A first-rate establishment!"

We had all begun to feel that even though the strange mixture of cold, malicious threats and bureaucratic order was oppressive, we were not in imminent danger in this prison. Lemke's accounts – the voice of experience of one who had already once spent four months in a place like this and had on the whole come through them just fine – had done their part to restore what courage we might have lost after the events at the Lipno train station. The murders and abuses which we had been told about must have been random cases… Later we learned that on this selfsame day, September 3, Bromberg had seen its day of bloodshed. It was a good thing that we did not know of these events at the time, for our home town was only a few hours away from Bromberg. We believed our loved ones to be safe; if we had known of the atrocities being committed on those left behind, these days of our imprisonment would hardly have been bearable for us.

We had spent the first night lying on the floor of the cattle cars or huddling on our suitcases, the second on the rattling boards of the panje carts; this night we hoped we could actually sleep through until morning. The straw sacks seemed to us more delicious a resting place than our beds at home, and our aching bones felt the relief of a softer padding. One must not forget that of all of us, Meister was probably the only one under forty years of age, and about half of us were over fifty.

The light was turned out around nine o'clock that night. Now it was dark in the cell, and we soon fell asleep. We were awakened several more times that night whenever newly arrived inmates were sent into our cell. Almost all of them were men we already knew, such as Reverend Duebal from Graudenz, the landowner Rust from Woiczin, and others. There was always a lively welcome. We saw how the new arrivals breathed more freely when they saw us, and how their confidence grew. They all had gone through some more or less fear-filled days, and we thought we could assure them that there would be no more overly horrible things in store for them here at the prison. Our Killer Senior, who had been a guest of this establishment for several months already, had told us a few things that served to reassure us.

Towards midnight, when we had once again had a half-hour's sleep, the lights were turned on again from the outside; we woke up and heard the key being turned in the lock. Killer Senior jumped off his bed-perch and roared an order, we got up and arranged ourselves in drowsy rows of two, the warden came in, and we bellowed our greeting: *"Dobra noc, panie przodowniku!"* Behind the Pole, a single man entered the cell, tall, wiry, slim, a man with nothing out-of-the-ordinary about him. He came in calmly and with embarrassed curiosity, and our Polish greeting visibly took him aback. Further, the air assaulting him in our hot, overcrowded room was not exactly roses. He opened his rather sleepy eyes for a surprised survey

and his nose wrinkled. I forgot where I was, and cried loudly:
"Man, Udo Roth!"

He looked at me, startled, then grinned and recognized me
despite my three days' growth of beard and lack of glasses. Delighted, we shook hands. Killer Senior, shocked by such a lack
of discipline, made move to separate us, but the przodownik
only grinned in magnanimous disdain and shuffled flat-footed
out the door again. He was probably tired too.

Udo Roth shook everyone's hand and, having understood
the situation right away and being thoroughly exhausted, he
took a straw sack from the ever-shrinking pile and made move
to lie down among us. Never in my life will I forget the
moment when he stood there before us, his left hand holding a corner of the sack hanging down to the floor behind
him, when he suddenly raised his right hand slightly and
said: "Gentlemen, they're already at the Vistula, coming from
Pomerania!"

It seemed to me as though we all staggered a little at that
moment. I felt my knees trembling, and had to sit down. A
stiff silence suddenly filled the room, but inside we were in
uproar. It was a good thing that our Killer Senior picked
that moment to say a few words to the vice-Starost, otherwise we would no doubt have forgotten ourselves. But even
so I couldn't help myself, I had to ask: "Udo, where?" It was
said quietly, and he, understanding right away, replied just as
quietly: "Near Kulm."

Measured by the course of the Vistula river that was some
120 kilometers away, but only 80 or so as the crow flies. Even
though we did not know the exact numbers, we all knew the

location of the larger cities and towns of our homeland. Now our thoughts stirred and longing awoke and there was probably not one among us who didn't try to calculate how much longer it might be before "they" would arrive in Hohensalza and then in Wloclawek. We had probably all assumed that the first advance would be through the Corridor in order to establish a connection with East Prussia. But now, belief had turned to certainty. I don't know how Udo Roth had heard the news. It was the only news to reach us during the entire time of our imprisonment. It strengthened us immeasurably.

Finally our overtired bodies demanded rest, and we all slept deeply and without dreams.

By Monday the population of our cell had grown to thirty-two men. Killer Senior told us that a second cell on the same floor as ours held another forty Germans. In the morning and around noon, the following days as well, we were always taken twelve men at a time to the wash room. Monday morning we were led into a large shower; we had to strip naked and soap up – partly ourselves, partly each other, depending on orders – and then got a lukewarm shower. Meanwhile our clothes were taken to be deloused in a steam-boiler which the German administration had evidently installed in this prison during the Great War, for the boiler bore an iron plaque with a German inscription. I recall it said "Main Delousing Facility" and the name of a city in the East.

We slept through the night from Monday to Tuesday without interruptions. We recovered our strength a little during those days, as we still had food and received enough water. Our Killer Senior saw to that; being an old-established inmate, he had a good relationship with one of our guards and was even able to smuggle a few boxes of cigarettes into our cell, for hefty payment of course.

Incidentally, the inmate who had shaved our heads was a brother-in-law of our trusty Killer, and, as the latter told us proudly, the women's section of the prison also housed a blood relative of his. One can see that he was from a very busy family.

On Monday the bomber alarm sounded repeatedly; through the two small windows we would hear the confused chatter of Polish anti-aircraft fire, which seemed very loud in our small cell. Bombs did not appear to have fallen that day; we suspected that it had been reconnaissance flights by our Luftwaffe.

On Tuesday around noon the sirens went off again. We knew that the German planes would not drop gas bombs and therefore refused to constantly close the two windows of our cell; one of us always had to climb onto the shoulders of a strong comrade to do so. Our three Poles, however – a Polish merchant had joined us in the meantime – always screamed and shrieked in fear, and so this time our comrade Harmel from Strelno decided to close the two hatches. Hardly had he climbed down again from Udo Roth's shoulders before we heard a deafening howl descending on us like a hammer blow from the sky, followed immediately by an explosion; the just-closed windows burst, a hail of small shrapnel sprayed over us, the entire old building shivered and shook, plaster crashed from the ceiling, large parts of the wall plaster also broke off and fell on us, and at the same time the room was bathed in a flickering red fire glow that turned the clouds of dust and dirt filling our cell into a reddish fog. When the glow had faded we saw through the windows some thick, toxic-black columns of smoke rising from the square outside. At that moment probably all of us thought the prison was on fire.

When the bomb fell I had sat near the doorway mending my stockings. My first reaction was to get away from the outside wall, to the pile of straw sacks. I took a flying leap to the other corner of the large room, stumbling in the process and tearing all the skin off the top of my toes on my right foot. The move had been about as fast as a soldier can throw himself to the ground when a grenade hits. Others dropped to the floor, still others leaped away from the outside wall like me, or at least into the room's corners, because the likelihood of the walls collapsing is less there. It was a massive confusion, and I think we all yelled or screamed in the first moment of shock. In any case I can attest that it is a horrible sensation to be locked up in the cell of a stone prison during an air raid.

Once the first excitement had died down we saw that Walter Milbradt lay bleeding beneath three other comrades. We went to help him but were distracted by a screeching, piercing, incessant screaming. Our Killer Senior clung like a spider monkey to one of the two windows, he clutched the iron bars with both hands and howled and screamed Polish prayers and half-sentences without seeming to pause for breath; we kept hearing the words *Matka boska, Matka boska!* and *Jaschka kochana, Jaschka kochana!* I have already mentioned that the Cell Senior was a short fellow. It was a mystery to all of us how he had managed so suddenly to reach the window, for as I said we others always had to climb onto another man's shoulders to open or close the hatches. Strangely enough, the sight of the writhing body, the squawking cries of the Pole calmed me down. No, I would not act as crazy as that.

Udo Roth bent forward and called, "come on, Harmel, get up, look out and check what's going on." Short, tough Harmel understood right away what Roth meant; he climbed up on his back and looked out the second window.

Now a man hung from each window. But while one shrieked and lamented, the other surveyed the scene outside on the square as best as possible and then gestured in calm dismissal. He climbed back down. A small wooden shed nearby was burning, he said, that was all.

Walter Lemke had been one of the first to regain his composure after the initial fright; he said – though he did speak a little more excitedly than usual – that the prison building was still standing and the cracks in the walls didn't seem bad enough to indicate an imminent collapse. So, quiet, everyone!

But we were far from quiet yet. The two other Poles which we had all but ignored until then were acting like madmen. A roar of screaming voices was to be heard from the neighboring cells, we heard inmates banging on the doors and also heard dull pounding blows from other parts of the building. Evidently the frightened prisoners were trying to batter down the cell doors with benches or wooden blocks. In one case they must have succeeded because suddenly we heard noise and shrieks of fear in the hallway and the sound of many running feet. Our Poles were seized by the same idea, they picked up the tabletop board and tried to ram down the door with it, all three of them together – for by then our Killer Senior had dropped from the window like an overripe apple, had scraped his hands and knees on the wall as he fell, and this had not served to calm him down. In a piercing voice used to giving orders, Udo Roth suddenly roared at the three of them like I have rarely heard a man roar, not even my sarge twenty years ago, and we grabbed the Polacks and forced them into a corner. We had no desire to break out and then be shot for it by the guards.

Finally the three Poles calmed down, but our Killer Senior was very quiet from that point on and the vice-Starost did not lose the crazed flicker in his eyes for hours. We swept up the fallen ceiling and wall plaster and the glass and waited to see what would happen. Our comrade Milbradt from Altreden had a deep cut from one of the glass shards; others were only slightly injured. After a time a guard appeared to assess the damage. He took the injured men with him and they returned half an hour later, properly bandaged. They told us that the Polish guards and the infirmary personnel were terrified beyond words and that the orderlies' hands had trembled while they bandaged the injured.

Even hours later, our cell was filled with a cloud of dust that settled so slowly that we had to keep our eyes, mouth and nose covered with handkerchiefs. Nonetheless we coughed and sneezed until well after dark.

In the evening we heard from one of the guards that the grenade had fallen about two meters away from the wall of our prison, into the square where it had collapsed the wall of the prison kitchen and cost our *"przodownik"* his life. We had to keep a tight rein on ourselves so as not to show our satisfaction at that bit of news. Aside from the first night, when he had tried to break us psychologically, the man had not harmed us. The bureaucratically ordered routine of prison life had not yet given him the opportunity. But all of us had dreaded the thought of being left in that man's hands if, perhaps, the approach of the battle zone incited the people's hatred of us even more and the regulations in place for our prison were once broken. To date, despite many a petty harassment, we had no cause for serious complaint; after all, Wloclawek was not one of the infamous Polish torture institutions such as Bereza Katuska or Sieradz.

We hoped for a quiet night. Since the grenade had damaged the electrical wiring, we had to lie down to sleep in total darkness; even this night our Killer Senior had not forgone his elevated bed on the tabletop.

4

Departure for the Sugar Factory

That night, fists suddenly pounded on our door, we heard an uproar and yelling in the hallways, a guard opened the cell and shone a candle into our room where we had all awoken with a start and stared at him, sitting on our straw sacks.

"Everyone out!" he yelled. "Alarm! Out, right now, line up in the square downstairs, move, move!" He entered the cell, yanked some of us to their feet and tried to shove them, half-dressed as they were, out into the corridor. But Udo Roth stepped in and said, in a controlled voice whose very calm brought the Poles a little to their senses, that we at least had to put our shoes on. To the constant impatient urging of the guard who specifically forbade us to take any of our few possessions, we finally stepped out into the utterly dark hallway, groped our way along the walls and thumped down the stairs. Three or four of our number had had the presence of mind to take one of the prison blankets with them; I myself had nothing more than a thin prison shirt, jacket and pants, socks and shoes, and the other comrades were dressed the same. Suspenders and belts had been taken from us.

We did not stand long in the square. In the light of stable lanterns we were arranged in rows of four. The Polish criminals who constituted the bulk of the prison's population were put at the end, so that now we even lost the company of our Killer Senior, and we were marched out the same wide gate through which we had marched in three nights before. A man in Polish uniform stood at the corner, we thought he was one of the prison wardens but in the dark it was impossible to be sure.

Walking beside me, short, tough, indomitable Lemke wanted to do something to lift our spirits. Besides, at that moment we all felt something akin to gratitude for the two days of relative peace we had spent in this prison. Lemke therefore said to the man at the corner as we marched past him out into the street, softly and in German: "Many thanks for your hospitality, good sir! We shall recommend your establishment to our friends."

His words prompted great merriment among us, which was heightened by the fact that we knew we could not dare laugh out loud. The relief of being out of the prison may have contributed to the lightening of our mood as well – in any case, stifled snorts of laughter kept pushing their way out among us for minutes on end. Those walking beside us would give us startled slaps on the shoulder, might even warn us to "hush up, man!", but they would then have a hard time keeping their own laughter down. Of course the guards noticed what was happening, but didn't know why we were so gleeful, and immediately began with threats. Their words returned us to grim reality. We'd see, they yelled, we'd see we had nothing to laugh about, they'd make sure of that, and we should take care. Some of them distributed punches and slaps among us. We quickly fell silent.

All of us knew what Poles were capable of, but still we were optimistic, overall.

We were amongst ourselves again, only Germans, we no longer felt spied on – for that was the only reason the three Poles had been put in our cell, to watch us – we again felt that we were in the honest company of comrades. Despite the uncertainty of our future it gave us new courage. And we needed courage. We all assumed that we had been removed so hastily from the city of Wloclawek – which now bears its ancient German name, Leslau, again – because our troops were approaching. It strengthened us, but it also showed that there would still be some bad days ahead. This was how we would always be removed from our advancing troops' reach; whenever we were close to being liberated, they would march off with us again – that's what we all thought, and some spoke their thoughts aloud. When one of us again did so, sounding rather miserable and fearful, I heard Walter Lemke, marching beside me, reply, softly so the Polish guards would not understand, but with strong emphasis: "Yes, but only until the day they are faster than we and the Poles!"

For anyone with poor eyesight the march was torture. Though it's true that even the comrades with good eyes could see next to nothing in the dark, still anyone who needs to wear glasses and has ever tried to find his way in the unfamiliar dark without them will know what a feeling of uncertainty it creates.

After about an hour we stopped at a forest edge; panje carts were waiting for us on the road. We were distributed equally among them, told to squat down on the boards, and a six-hour ride began. At that point all of us, even our most aged comrades, would have preferred to continue on foot, for on the bad roads we were constantly shaken until our teeth rattled. Really it is wrong to say that we sat on the carts; rather, we were continually flung into the air, sometimes higher, sometimes not as high, to land equally harshly each time on the boards on our posterior that soon passed sore. To increase the discomfort, the boards, which ran the length of the cart and also formed its floor, also banged and snapped up and down in a rhythm all their own. After only half an hour every bone hurt, our bodies were totally shaken out of order, and our stomachs were no longer where they should be.

It won't be hard to understand that, being men in only other men's company, we did not censor our speech. Especially later on, when we had all realized that we were constantly in danger of a painful death, we resorted to a kind of front-lines talk whose strongest fount was not only a stoic disregard of our surroundings but also the determination to counter the Poles' hatred with equanimity. But at the same time it's understandable that a rattling cart and a painful posterior are not the best prerequisites for proud and calm composure. Walter Lemke, who rode on the same cart as me, suddenly said:

"Hey, Reinhold, tell me, what are those monkeys with the naked red butt?"

Since my selfsame butt was hurting as badly as never since my early childhood, when my father or teacher had tanned it thoroughly for some silly boyish prank, I grumbled back in a pretty bad mood: "Man, why? Baboon, I think. Or, no, wait: mandrill! Yes, they're called mandrills!"

"Well, then," he said with a cheerful growl, "if this keeps up for another hour I'll be a mandrill."

Suppressed laughter filled our cart again. Of course it did not last long, for the ride continued for another five hours.

The September nights of 1939 were cold under clear starry skies. As dawn approached the cold grew bitter, and we shivered badly in our thin clothes. In the end we huddled together, shivering silently, and the shaking and rattling of the cart, throwing us every which way and against each other, now served to warm us a little.

As the sun rose in the east to the left of our road, behind a stand of those tall ragged poplars that are characteristic of former Russian Poland, we saw the first of our convoy of carts stop. We pulled up close to the first cart and stopped as well. We had arrived. Some large red buildings seemed to grow out of the landscape, surrounded by a high exterior wall. As we found out later, it was the sugar factory of Chodsen.

When we disembarked we had to lift old man Heinecke, with his heart condition, down from his cart. He was stiff with exhaustion, did not speak or move, and we feared that he would die in our hands. But once he had felt firm ground under his feet for half a minute, he opened his eyes and looked around. Slowly an awareness of his and our situation returned. He moaned in a weak raspy voice and tried to walk; it must have been painful – for a moment the look in his old eyes was almost one of despair. But when he saw our concern his demeanor changed; the old gentleman's eyes flashed at us, and suddenly he said in a voice almost as strong as before: "Well, let's go!" He moved his legs, and it worked; slowly and with difficulty, but better with each passing step. Nonetheless it may have been his salvation that we had to wait in the ditch for a few minutes first, and were permitted to sit down. When we got underway, two comrades supported him on either side.

There seemed to be no end to the walk. Our bodies ached – all our limbs, arms no less than legs and back – brain and stomach were shaken through and through – and when we were told to stop outside a small brick house we felt as though we had marched two or three kilometers with heavy luggage.

(A few weeks later Walter Lemke and I went back to look at this place again. We could hardly believe that the stretch of road we had walked was actually no more than one hundred and fifty meters, at most. We walked it over and over again, tried to determine locations and to recognize the buildings, we asked Polish inhabitants of the hamlet who had witnessed our arrival as described – but it was correct, the road was no longer than that. It wasn't until then that we realized fully how exhausted, disoriented and battered we had been at that time.)

We had to wait again here, and again we were herded into the ditch to do so. Ahead of us was a building which we thought was the police station, and behind and beside it were the grounds of the sugar factory. Behind us, the side street was lined with several low, single-family homes surrounded by gardens sporting autumn colors.

While we sat thus in the ditch, more new transports of ethnic Germans arrived from the main country road. Since we had been the first to arrive at the building, our guards wanted to be the first to be checked in, and so they sent the new arrivals to our left wing. As a result every new group was led past us.

The very first group that was herded past us showed us that our time in Wloclawek prison had been a stay in paradise. A farmer and his wife walked at the head of the group, carrying a large laundry basket between them, covered with a cloth. The man's right hand was handcuffed to his neighbor's left. He was a strong, stocky fellow whose face was covered in big dark blotches; his left ear was crusted with blood. He walked past us with heavy, shuffling steps without raising his eyes from the ground, and we saw that he was dragging one leg. His wife, with a round white face under masses of brown hair – I still see her in my mind as though it were now – stared straight ahead, wide-eyed, while tears coursed down her face.

In the middle of the road directly before us stood a policeman with a pince-nez and goatee. It will be a long time before I will forget the crow of his voice. He watched the new arrivals approach, and when the man and wife stopped before him – since he did not move out of the way – he pointed with a thick willow switch to the basket and asked what it contained. In a trembling voice the woman replied that their child was in it, an infant, but that it was asleep. The commissar hesitated, and for a moment we who were watching in breathless suspense thought we saw a trace of embarrassment and human compassion on his face. But he swung the willow rod and barked: "Take the cloth off."

The couple set the basket down and the mother removed the cloth. We had stood up to look in as well. The basket did in fact contain a child, perhaps six months old, lying on some pillows. But something about the position of the sleeping child must have struck the mother as odd, she bent over it, and with a low cry that made my heart tremble she took its arm. Then the woman snatched her daughter up, falling to her knees. The child was dead. And while the farmer's wife clutched the little corpse to her breast as if turned to stone, and made no sound at first, her husband began to sob uncontrollably. And the man's crying was even worse than the woman's stiff silence. The guards screamed at the two of them to move on, and the woman obeyed; she walked past us like a sleepwalker, still pressing the child's body close. Her husband, manacled to his neighbor, pulled her close to him with his left, put his free arm around her and stumbled, staggering and sobbing, along the street. Only now that his will to endure had been broken, we saw how badly he limped. And we also realized what the dark blotches on his face were; he had been beaten with fists and probably also with hard objects, and blood pooling under his skin had marked him thus. Two comrades walking behind the couple took up the basket and carried it away.

Some fifty Germans were in this group. More than half of

them showed visible signs of maltreatment, several had blood-soaked bandages around their head or hands. A gray-haired old man had his right arm in a sling. We saw that they had all bandaged themselves, for they had clearly torn shirts and other articles of clothing to make something with which to stem the flow of blood.

Men and women from the town of Kruschwitz passed by. I recognized *Rentmeister* (administrator) Ortwich, a calm, matter-of-fact man. He was staggering back and forth like a drunk. Walking behind him was a farmer I did not know, being supported on either side by two others. A hoarse voice behind me spoke: "My God – that's Witt... he's been shot in the side!" I could not see it, but Lemke insisted that he had clearly seen the gunshot wound. It turned out later that he had seen correctly. And suddenly I felt a hand clutching my forearm. I had seen it too: a young girl, eighteen or twenty years of age, was walking behind Adolf Witt. Her head was wrapped in a completely blood-soaked bandage clearly intended to support her jaw. "Reinhold, Reinhold, that's his daughter," Lemke groaned. And at that moment we knew far from the whole story. Three members of the Witt family had been shot to death; the mother lay at home, gravely injured. Father and daughter were herded past us here, wounded.

One young fellow carried an old man past us, with white hair, stiff as a wooden figurine, as though he had just been taken off a crucifix. "Old man Diesing. He's more than seventy-five years old!" Lemke's voice was hoarse in my ear. I saw the old man's face, it was lifeless, and looking out of his eyes was the indifference of a man who sees his death approaching and has come to terms with it.

Thus the prisoners filed past us, staggering, silent, looking straight ahead or down at the ground. Hardly any of them ever looked to the side where we lined the ditch, bearded and with shaven heads. Anyone who could not continue was forcibly driven on by the guards with punches and blows from rifle butts. Woe to anyone who made a move that might have been taken for resistance! The policemen hit such unfortunates over the head or neck without so much as batting an eye. Not far from me, a young man received such a blow that he slowly sank to his knees and could not go on. But the comrade walking to his right pulled him up, another from the row behind them leaped forward and lifted him onto the first man's back, and the latter walked on, carrying the unconscious man while the policeman sauntered alongside, mocking them.

At that moment an uproar ensued to our right, perhaps twenty meters away. We heard the guards roaring and another voice pleading. In the confusion we could not make out the words or see exactly what was going on, we could only tell that several men had been forced out of their row by the guards. Suddenly the air was rent by a piercing scream of terror, it was a very high voice that cracked and then broke off, and then we heard two shots. The column just being marched past us panicked, everyone began to run, to rush past us, the guards yelled and rained blows on our terrified disoriented comrades, more shots rang out, and now we saw two men lying on the ground under the arch of a gateway and five or six men in uniform standing around them. Two of them grabbed the shot men and dragged them into the yard. We did not see them again.

A terrible silence reigned in our small group. I could not bear to look at any of them. I had clenched both fists and rested my head on them, sitting in the ditch trembling with indescribable rage. I did not notice until much later that even though it was a cold foggy September morning I was bathed in sweat. Later, body and soul had become so dulled that they responded only tiredly to such events.

A new convoy of fellow-sufferers arrived on the main road. They too were herded onto the side road and past us. Several women walked at its head. I noticed an older peasant woman, she carried herself with unbroken will and did not have the same desperate or helpless air that many of our women showed. The corners of her mouth held something like disdain. She was also one of the few who looked closely at all of us. She was wearing wooden slippers; they had not even given her enough time to put on proper footwear.

We saw boys and girls, seven to ten years of age, walking along holding their father's or mother's hand. We saw a woman carrying an infant in her arms. We saw one group of men, almost all of whom had injured, bleeding hands. They had been made to lie on their stomachs on the ground, stretch out their arms over their heads, and the Poles – we learned all this later, from the abused men themselves – the Poles, wearing nailed boots, had stomped back and forth over the backs of their victims' hands. Not a few of them had sustained broken fingers or knuckles. We saw several fellow Germans whose age we could not estimate because their faces were so swollen from countless blows and so darkened by the blood pooling under their skin that there was not a white or even a pale spot to be seen; these people gave the impression of being Negroes. We saw an old white-haired man who was so badly beaten that he could no longer walk on his feet. Two neighbors had linked their arms with his on either side and were dragging him past us, while he tried to make it easier for them by crawling through the sand on the street on his knees. This group, which brought up the staggering rear of the marching column, was accompanied by two young Poles no older than seventeen or eighteen, who urged them to greater speed with howls and jeers; these brutal fellows beat the old invalid's two helpers with switches as thick as their thumbs. But the samaritans did not leave the old man, they dragged him on.

Our own guards, who had still showed a hint of pity when they saw the dead child in the laundry basket, had been caught up in the general madness that characterized these Poles. They had joined the other guards in yelling at the people staggering past, they screamed in approval, cheered and howled, give it to the Hitler-swine, the rotting dog corpses, the spies, the cholerras, the filthy Germans, give it to them! They yelled at us, look, watch, this is what will happen to all you Hitlerists, this is how we'll do it to all of you, all of you have to die like dogs, you'll see!

Meanwhile, men and women, young fellows and girls, even children had emerged from the houses of the small settlement around the sugar factory, and it was gruesome to see how even ten- and twelve-year-olds joined in with the mob's howling and cursing and the hate-filled cheering. But to give the truth its due, I also saw the horrified eyes of a ten-year-old girl who suddenly stood, pale-faced, at the opposite edge of the road and then ran away sobbing when a woman, who had tried in her terror to hide in a lilac bush off to our right, was routed by the police and hounded past us with punches, kicks and blows from rifle butts.

The sight of the poor comrades trudging past us, of the men and women and children who were Germans like us, kindled a passionate sense of unity and a common bond in us; even the lowest, no matter how dull and sluggish he might be in his thoughts and feelings, now knew what it meant to have a Fatherland – now that it was so far from us. The sullying of our honor which we had to endure without defense filled us with a tired horror. Many, many among us would have had the strength to step forward and say: Stop! Shoot us if you must, but stop this! But they would not have been shot, they would have been beaten down, pounded with punches and kicks, spat on, cursed – and no-one managed to take that on himself voluntarily. That went beyond what we could take. The violation of dignity, the desecration of all things human that the Polish nation committed there right before our eyes while demeaning and besmirching itself in such an unspeakable, incomprehensible way – that robbed us of the last of our strength. Dully, we watched the spectacle before us. I could not form a clear thought, and my comrades felt the same. Grief, shame, dismay, fear, pity and horror weighed on us, and no-one could bear it with the strength of his soul intact.

Now we all knew what was in store for us, but even that could no longer frighten us very much.

5

In the Factory Yard

We had waited for two or perhaps three hours when finally the policeman with the pince-nez appeared again and called our names. We had to line up on the road, were re-grouped and then led as the first of all of us into the yard of the factory. At first we thought the factory had been bombed by German planes, but soon we learned that it had just not been used for a few years. The yard was separated from the road by a high barbed-wire fence and, in some places, by a red brick wall. Guards were posted everywhere. We were led up to a long, tall building, evidently an old sugar warehouse, but were not permitted to enter; instead, we were assigned places along one of the two broad sides of the structure. And that's where we were left to camp out. Not a soul saw to us all day long, and we got no food and no water. Since the day was warm it was quite bearable. Some of us had a few leftovers of rations, which were distributed among our group as fairly as possible. But in the noonday heat our thirst grew worse and worse. I picked a guard who seemed to have a humane demeanor and asked him if we would be given anything to eat or drink. The man replied that of course we would get food, after all, the Poles are not barbarians. But this promise, made by other Poles as well, was all we received.

In the afternoon someone said that coffee was being brewed in a corner of the yard. Some of us managed to get hold of some cups. Since hundreds of people crowded around the iron pot that had been set up in a shed, and the Poles did not dream of ensuring order, there was not much to be done. Anyone who managed to get a cupful shared it, sip and sip alike, with the rest. These past days had taught us what comradeship is. The word was never spoken among us, but each learned from the other, none wanted to come up short, and the example set by Udo Roth and Walter Lemke worked on all of us. I also cannot forget to mention old man Stübner; even later, during our great march, he often refused bread and water altogether, saying that others needed it more than he did. Old man Heinecke, the young brave Wilhelm Meister, sly Julius Mutschler who often managed to find something edible, be it a few turnips, some sour pickles or two cups of buttermilk, and delivered it all faithfully to Lemke – all of them did what they could, and their tenacity, their eagerness to help, their willing sacrifices, all done as if it were a matter of course, made my heart beat faster with pride and joy many a time.

When we had entered the factory yard there had not been a single other German in it. Only a few hours later the place was teeming with people, and convoy after convoy of tired, frightened prisoners arrived. All of them were assigned to spots in the open air, and soon we were told to move closer together. We already knew how cold the September nights were getting, and gladly moved as close together as we could so as to be able to keep each other warm in the coming night.

As the afternoon went on, we all grew ever more hungry. Yes, we had been fed in prison, and in our cell where we had not had any exercise the food had seemed almost enough. But here in the open air it turned out that we were really quite debilitated.

Trying to be as inconspicuous as possible, I wandered around among the new arrivals and the groups already encamped, even though the guards had forbidden it. But we were always looking uneasily for friends and acquaintances. Whenever one recognized someone there was always much to tell; it passed the time and one did not heed one's rumbling stomach as much. Soon, Wilhelm Meister joined me.

As I already mentioned, the square where we were confined was surrounded by a barbed-wire fence. I had heard that the women were also being kept in the same factory yard, but separated from us by barbed wire. I ambled slowly through the groups of our men, standing around or encamped as the case might be, and in fact found the women in an enclosure of their own. Cautiously we approached the barbed wire fence behind which they were settled. Meister called to a girl standing near the wire. She came towards us right away, but pretended to just walk up and down the fence; without looking at us, with her face half averted, she asked if she should get us something to eat. I told her she should keep her supplies, as none of us knew what was to come. At that, she dared a glance in our direction, smiled, and said that if we had money she would try to buy some bread and fruit for us. They were not kept under as close a guard as the men were.

Neither of us had money but we knew that one of our comrades had managed to keep a larger sum hidden from the Poles. Meister hurried back, while I now observed that on the opposite side the women's enclosure bordered on a road and that there was only a wooden fence there. Behind that, she told me, were the Jews; at first they had tried to curse and harass the women but once they had realized that they might be able to do some business with them they had instantly become very obliging.

We talked a little, and agreed that if a guard were to try to chase me away I would claim that the girl was my daughter. After Meister returned with money we soon had an entire loaf of bread, a bag of apples and even a piece of sausage. A few women had gathered together in a group and stood in such a way that the guards could not see the exchange. Another woman even obtained two bottles of lemonade for us. They were rolled under the fence with a vigorous shove. Similar barter was going on at other points along the fence as well. Meister had soon made friends with the girl – and truly it was a joy just to look at her. Her spirit was completely unbroken, and in her delight at being able to help us she laughed so that her entire healthy fresh young face lit up. When we said good-bye we promised to return soon.

I could not do so that day; on our way back to our place in the yard, when we had passed the short end of the first sugar warehouse, we saw in the long narrow space between it and the adjoining building how a young boy, no older than fifteen, dressed only in a bloody gym shirt and black bathing trunks, was being chased back and forth by half a dozen crazed, bayonet-wielding guards. The boy made not a sound, and perhaps this was exactly what enraged the guards so much. The hounded young boy tried repeatedly to break out at either end of the narrow space forty meters or so in length, but failed. Evidently the Poles had singled him out and then beaten him, for his face was swollen and suffused with blood, and his naked legs were also bleeding from multiple bayonet stab wounds. But the boy refused to give up, and eventually he managed to outmanoeuvre the Poles who kept trying to force him towards the middle; he broke through, ran as fast as he could down the narrow space to the end farthest from us, and darted around the side of the warehouse, the Poles cursing and hard on his heels. But they could no longer get him; his minimum of clothing was his salvation now as the uniformed Poles in their tall boots could not keep up, and he disappeared into the crowd that had gathered. Some quick-witted comrade must have lent him a jacket, probably also a cap and pants, and his pursuers lost him in the crowd.

The two of us stood boxed in between some comrades we did not know. They were dead silent, and then turned away with faces like frozen masks. I had not noticed before now that along the wall of one of these warehouses, lining the sort of corridor where the manhunt had just taken place, a row of completely apathetic men sat on the ground. All of them had clearly endured horrific maltreatment, most of them wore bloody shirts, their faces were beaten black and blue and their heads were crusted with blood.

A moment ago we had been full of optimism on our way back to our group. Now we arrived there in crushed silence and gave the food we had bartered to Walter Lemke, who distributed it among all of us. I ate, for I reminded myself that I would yet need a lot of strength. But I had a hard time choking down the bread and fruit that only a short time ago had tempted me as the epitome of a lavish feast. Then I got up. I could not sit still, and wandered restlessly around the yard. Lemke joined me and I told him what we had just witnessed. I was trembling with rage and fear alike.

"We have to do something about it, we can't just sit around helpless while they butcher us! We have to get some weapons!"

Lemke was as pale as a sheet but kept a calm exterior. That wouldn't help at all, he said; they were only waiting for us to defend ourselves, and then they would shoot us all – and if not, they would pick every tenth of us, and the misery would only grow and grow without us having helped whoever they chose to target next.

We debated back and forth. Udo Roth joined us as well. Eventually we had to part, for we found no solution; there was nothing to be done but to bear it all with patience. "There is one thing we can do: never ever show fear! Never let them see even the slightest bit of fear. Prepare yourselves that they may shoot you or beat you to death, but then die fearlessly. These dogs will not hear me whimper." Roth's lips twisted as he said it, but I knew he would keep his word.

So I walked away aimlessly through the crowd, but turned

back right away. I had heard Udo Roth's voice: "For God's sake, Pastor!" Roth stood facing someone I could not recognize from the distance. I pushed my way back to them. Every fibre of my being fought against seeing even more, but the wish to not deliberately close my eyes to the truth won out. All of us were as though cursed with the need to find out more and ever more. Udo Roth was speaking with a man of average stature, whose face looked like the many we had already seen. It was black from countless blows, his eyes were almost swollen shut, lips cracked and bleeding, blood crusted at his temples. We led him to our group and sat him down on the thin layer of straw there. Every move must have been painful, but he saw our horrified faces, he felt our shock, and smiled to ease our worry. He did not complain as he told us of his journey, and it was moving to see how his unbroken spirit strengthened many of our comrades.

It was Pastor Mix from Strelno; the Poles had regarded him and all his fellow clergymen as a particularly dangerous stronghold of all things German. And it is indeed a fact that the Protestant Church in Poland was one of the most unshakeable supports of the German people in my homeland. The Protestant clergymen, therefore, were targeted particularly harshly; Pastor Mix, who had to endure the entire march of the following days from beginning to end, died in Lodz of the inhuman abuses he in particular was subjected to over and over again, but he lived long enough to see our hour of liberation.

Another one to join us here in our imprisonment that afternoon was Senator Dr. Busse from Tupadly, a man more than seventy years old, who had so often represented the German ethnic group and their rights in the Polish Senate, a calm and courageous champion of our people. The Poles had taken a special interest in him, naturally. The old gentleman had to be carried into the camp by comrades as he could no longer walk. He had been treated almost even more viciously than Pastor Mix, and we all feared that he would not survive the night. But our women got us a few refreshments for him and it helped a little. Thanks to the wonderful spirit of one-for-all that reigned among us, he made it to Lowicz and later even to Lodz, and we may hope that he will yet spend many happy years in our liberated homeland and watch its resurrection.

6

In the Sugar Warehouse

Evening came. I could not take Lemke's and Roth's well-meant advice to lie down and sleep. My inner unrest was far too great. And so I got up to wander around the large factory yard where other comrades were walking around just like me, or stood silently in small groups. It was even more dangerous to do so now than during the day. If a guard had seen me, I would have been given a beating at the very least.

At the door to one of the sugar warehouses someone suddenly, questioningly, called me by name. I saw a man I could not recognize in the dark, even though I stepped close to him. I remembered once again how I had been relieved of my glasses. It turned out that I had met Bruno Schneider, the leading official of a large estate near Hohensalza. Delighted, we began to talk; as in all these conversations, we immediately recounted what had happened to us. In our eagerness to share our news we did not realize that more and more comrades were crowding around us, and they in turn could not know that I did not belong to their group. It was dark all around us. The entire group suddenly began to move, involuntarily I moved along with them, until suddenly I found myself standing right at the door of the warehouse. The two halves of the iron gate had been swung back just enough to make an opening at most half a meter in width; two guards each were posted to the right and left of this opening. I shied away, tried to step back, the guards roared at me, I called back that I was not even part of the warehouse group, but at that they descended on me, the other prisoners behind me became frightened and pushed me forward, I protested, received a harsh blow to my back that sent me staggering forward, in the dark I saw a rifle butt swung towards me, tried to evade it, found myself being dragged forward, and that was my salvation. "Come on, man, you can leave tomorrow morning!" Schneider had grabbed me in a powerful grip and dragged me into the building. Outside the guards were yelling, the last of the small group crowded in, pale as ghosts, and then the gates were swung closed and the opening was sealed. I was locked up in the sugar warehouse.

We knew that many Germans had been locked into these two large brick structures for days already, and we had also heard about the awful conditions said to exist in there, but because the doors were always under guard and none of us engaged a Pole in conversation unnecessarily or even came near them, since one was only ever cursed obscenely for it, I had only heard third- or fourth-hand accounts.

Now I stood in one of these warehouses myself. A wave of used-up air, a wall of stench hit me in the face, foul-smelling vapors of urine and worse, of sweat and toilet effluvium, and half-unconscious I turned back and pounded with my fists against the iron gate through which I had just been shoved in. But again Schneider pulled me back. "They'll beat you to a pulp, come on now, there's nothing to be done about it!" He took me by the arm and pulled me away from the entrance, and I followed in a daze. It took all my self-control not to give in to the choking urge to vomit.

Ahead of me – he had let go of my arm again – Schneider walked down a narrow aisle running down the center of the huge hall. Crowded rows of men of all ages squatted to the left and right of it. Their faces were dull, the looks they gave me, indifferent. I felt as though I were walking through a colony of sloths; every move these people made was unbelievably slow, dragging. Their faces were pale and drained. Some of them slept, cramped into a ball as small as they could make themselves, others on their back and with mouth wide open; still others had burrowed into the straw or at least covered their head with a jacket, a hat, a blanket, trying not to see or hear; many rasped and moaned in their sleep; others huddled together, talking softly or staring silently at each other. A pale fog of sticky miasma lay over the entire scene and the sharp scent of half-rotted straw enhanced the rest of the malodorous mixture that passed for air. Together with the dust stirred up by the many passing feet, it crept into one's airways, clung to one's mucous membranes, dried out one's tongue and soon formed a bitter crust on one's lips.

Schneider led me to his place in the second-to-last row from the outside wall. The occupants already there willingly moved over, and I sat down on the stone floor covered only by a thin layer of filthy straw. Right away my neighbor addressed me by name, and I recognized *Rentmeister* Ortwich, whom I had seen arrive that morning. We began to talk about our experiences to date, and as always the first question was about our friends and relatives. Schneider gestured silently at a man lying four or five places over from us. At the distance I could not recognize him. "Old man Diesing!" Ortwich said softly. "He just lies there, barely moving. If he could have spent the day outside, lying in the sun, we might have got him back on his feet. He's a little better already. The ride on the cart all but did it for him. It's ninety kilometers from Kruschwitz to here."

I reached into my pocket where I had a lemon that I had jealously guarded until now. "Give him this. He should suck on it. Maybe it'll help." The yellow fruit was passed over and I saw how one of his neighbors bent over the prostrate figure and held it to his lips over and over.

Gradually time passed with talking and observation, and eventually I ceased to notice the semisolid air in which I was sitting.

The hall was approximately sixty to seventy meters long and perhaps eighteen to twenty meters wide. Eight hundred people inhabited it. Schneider had counted the rows; each row had between eighty and eighty-five people, and there were ten rows, five on either side of the center aisle. The air vents in the room had been boarded shut or plugged with rags. In the entire huge hall there was only one open window, perhaps half a square meter in size. Opening the remaining windows was forbidden. The warehouse was locked from dusk until dawn and no-one was permitted to leave. In the morning groups of ten men were let out into the factory yard for ten minutes. They had to line up in rows of two. From early in the morning the center aisle was full of people from end to end; since only sixty people were let out per hour, it theoretically took twelve hours for everyone to get out once. Four to five hours was the average wait time. But far too many couldn't wait that long. The straw had been piled a little higher in the corners, and anyone for whom the wait was too long had to answer the call of nature in a corner on the bare stone floor.

At first the Poles had locked men and women together in these warehouses; by the time I arrived, the women had been separated and moved to another building. It was an example of malicious torment with a particularly low motive.

The rest of us spent our nights outside, so why could the Poles not simply have left the doors to these two warehouses open so the prisoners could go in and out as needed? The entire grounds were fenced in with barbed wire, countless armed guards stood at the ready, a lieutenant had announced that machine guns were in position on the roofs of the factory buildings – so why did they need this special prison within the prison?

I must not forget to mention that the latrine that had been dug for us on the factory square was located right next to the wire fence that divided us from the women, and the women's corresponding facility was also right near the fence. Therefore we and our women had to exhibit to each other, as it were, those activities which everyone normally keeps private.

Further, the wooden fence from which the Jews watched us was also right nearby.

I had been a half hour at my new place in the sugar warehouse and had tried to get used to the idea of staying until morning amongst this teeming mass of dully staring, sleeping, or tiredly wandering people when suddenly a horrible scream rang through the hall, a long-drawn-out cry in which fear and animal rage warred for predominance in dreadful tones. There was suddenly a dead silence in the huge hall, those sleeping or dozing on the straw sat up, pale-faced, but before anyone could even ask or say anything, the same piercing voice rang out again from the same spot. It cried in German:

"Kill him, beat him to death, the damned dog!"

Horror gripped my throat. But now we heard other voices, four or five people all spoke at once, and then a clear and very calm deep voice carried through the hall: "Stay where you are, comrades, go back to sleep. Someone was just dreaming here. We woke him up, there's nothing to worry about." From the tone of the voice I could tell that the comrade who had said this was deliberately speaking longer than necessary so that the explanation he gave so calmly could ease the fear that had seized everyone after that horrible scream. But I saw eyes around me shining feverishly, and sure enough it was only a few seconds before there was a hoarse, stunned cry: "My God, my God, how will all this end, what are they going to do to us, not one of us is going to get out of here alive!" The voice died down into soft sobbing, it sounded like a woman's weeping but there were only men in this hall. A harsh voice said, loud and firm: "Shut up, man, pull yourself together. All of us will get out alive, we've done nothing wrong, we are innocent and unarmed. Don't drive the others crazy."

Schneider took my arm, I looked over at him and followed a gesture of his hand with my eyes. Four men were walking through the rows of the resting prisoners to the corner where the screaming had come from. They were prison inmates from Wloclawek, Schneider told me, they were placed with the Germans here and had already made all sorts of nasty threats. "All of you need to have your throats cut," they had said. "Just wait until the march begins, you'll see." And then, Schneider said, they had followed up with those same epithets I had no doubt also heard: Hitler-swine, traitors, dog corpses...

"Now they're going to ensure order over there!" he whispered. "Be careful. There are more of their kind in here."

In the uncertain light of the lamp the four who had got up to "ensure order" pushed ruthlessly through the figures lying or huddling on the floor, they stepped on or kicked the occasional one, there were harsh words, they replied with threats. I could not see clearly what was happening, but ever since I had been deprived of my glasses it seemed as though another sort of sense had developed. Foggily, I saw a man jerking up from the floor, there was roaring and yelling as the inmates had run into other criminals whom they seemed to have mistaken for Germans, and suddenly a wild fight was raging. It was strange: voices of jeering agitation and incitement chimed in from all sides in Polish, as did angry shouts of "quiet!", but silence fell amongst the Germans. They let the Poles beat each other up, and watched as they made up again later, but everywhere, the Germans laid back down on their thin layer of dirty straw to sleep – even those who had wandered around restlessly until then.

That night, in a bout of despair, Karl Lehr from Kruschwitz tried to commit suicide by slitting his throat with a knife he had borrowed from a neighbor. He was prevented in his endeavor by Dr. Studzinski, a doctor from Graudenz, German through and through despite his Polish name; the doctor read Lehr the riot act and then carefully bandaged him up. The next morning, Lehr staggered around the hall as if delirious. We feared that he would die, but he recovered and lived to see his home again.

The unbreathable air in that room, the feeling of being mercilessly locked up and cut off from the outside world, hunger and thirst – all this gnawed at the powers of resistance of these eight hundred people who were stacked beside each other so many like pieces of driftwood, who never got to see a Polish officer or higher-ranking police official whom one could have asked anything or made a complaint to. The boorish guards at the door knew nothing and replied to all questions with curse words or even punches.

The night passed uneasily. Nightmares shuddered through the souls of the sleepers. Pain and confusion gave rise to ever more fearful specters. They felt abandoned, beyond all help, defenseless in the hands of a hateful mob. Even those who could draw on defiance and strength of soul during their waking hours were at the mercy of natural fears while they slept. Whispers, bare breath of words, floated shivering through the stuffy air, drowned out every now and again by a sudden shriek of terror or by an uncontrolled whimper that spoke of naked, trembling fear. The people tossed and turned on the straw; sleep was not a kind friend to them, it amplified their torment. And over it all, the hazy evaporate from this mass of people hung heavily like a malodorous fog.

I slept little that night. I was plagued by terrible imaginings and fears and yet not willing to surrender into a sleep that would give complete power to the vague terrors that beset me. For as long as I was awake, I was master of my words, and strove to remain master of my thoughts as well. But my eyes burned with exhaustion.

Eventually I must have fallen asleep after all, for I woke with a start from a deep unconsciousness. A wild noise had woken me. In waking I felt as though I was choking, floating in muddy water laced with slimy snares, and had to fight for air and light. I even almost went through the motions of swimming to free myself from the seething uproar swirling around me, from the terrible specters and the whirling of dust and stench.

Schneider called to me, he said it was beginning, we had to line up, we were to be marched off. And then he grabbed me by the shoulders: "We're running away again already! The Prussians are coming, man, the Prussians, what else could it be! Hurry, man, come on!"

I leaped to my feet. The huge hall was filled with yelling, noise, a seething hubbub of shouting, running people. From the few windows, narrow rays of the crack of dawn quietly traced their lightened patterns across the bedlam in the room. The guards screamed and roared. The alarm call must have only just been given, but the crowd had answered with a single united shout.

The agitation settled quickly. While the first few groups already left the hall through the large iron gate, we stood waiting and watching. It was important to find out what the Poles planned to do with us and how we had best act. I had only one desire, to find my way back to my group, and I resolved to do it as cleverly as I could.

7

Marching, Marching Without End

It was much easier than I had expected. When we walked out through the gate, which unlike the previous night had now been flung open wide, we saw dense damp fog hanging over the yard; it was a bitterly cold morning, probably around five o'clock. Hundreds of people milled about in front of the gate; there was no order whatsoever. Schneider was standing next to me. I pressed his hand firmly. Ortwich was nowhere to be seen and I had no time to look for him. I had to take advantage of these moments of upheaval. I groped and pushed my way through the throng. From some large stains on the outside of the warehouse wall I could tell that I was near the spot used by my group, but without my glasses I could not recognize anyone from the distance.

Suddenly a familiar voice called me by name. "You too!" the voice added. "Of course. All the quality among us ends up here." Before me stood a tall blond man with a bushy beard and shabby, dirty clothes. He had his arm around the shoulders of a boy some fourteen years at most, who clung to him confused and frightened and watched the turmoil around him with huge eyes. More by his voice than by his face I recognized Herrn von Rosenstiel from Lipie. The two stood before me like a pair of wood-cut altar figures, and I will never forget how Rosenstiel held the boy close to him as though trying to protect him from all the dangers threatening him here. But we did not have the chance to converse at all, because suddenly I heard my name being called.

"Where? Where?" I heard. "There he is, over there, with Rosenstiel!" Lemke, Udo Roth, old man Stübner and Wilhelm Meister – all of them rushed towards me, shook my hand like someone they had believed dead, pounded on my shoulders, laughed and shouted all at the same time. Some guards took notice of us; Lemke grabbed my arm and dragged me away, back to the group I had belonged to. They were already lined up ready to march off.

At first I did not understand what they were so excited and happy about, and they must have seen my bafflement. Udo Roth whispered to me: "You were barely gone last night when they shot Reverend Reder. Here on our square." I asked for details, but none knew more than the bare fact itself. Later it turned out that in the time right before the outbreak of the war Reverend Reder had been on vacation. He had spent it near Danzig, outside Poland. That's where he was served his arrest papers. He cut his vacation short, drove back to his home town and reported to the Polish authorities, was arrested on the spot, carried off with the rest of us – and here he had paid the ultimate price for his loyalty to his German congregation.

We knew none of this at that time. I had not known Reverend Reder; we had been dulled by events and accepted his fate like all the other news. What was in store for us now was more important than what was past.

At first that morning we were very cold; we hopped from one foot to the other, pounded each other on the back, beat our arms. We were overtired, hungry, chilled to the bone, our bodies had no reserves of warmth, and we did not warm up until the sun finally burned the fog away. It turned into a very hot day. But with the warmth came exhaustion; standing in the sun, we would all have loved to get some sleep.

Suddenly, under that bright blue sky, a deep silence fell over us. No-one spoke, no-one hopped around or beat his arms. A low hum could be heard above us, coming closer quickly, and now everyone could hear the airplane soaring down at us from out of the silence in wide loops like a silver lark. Its still wings flashed in the morning sun, it was already large and clearly visible but came lower and even lower. "I can see the crosses," a trembling, hoarse voice said beside me. Then a shadow fell over us, the engines thundered across our upturned faces, we did not dare to move a hand or raise a cry. But if the silent cry of our hearts had been audible it would have drowned out the roar of the engines up there above us.

The airplane raced away like thunder above us, disappeared behind the trees lining the main road, and only now we heard that the Poles were screaming and raging; only now our ears registered that a few shots had been fired – but there it already came again, a little higher than before, the machine tilted sideways a bit and we thought we could make out a face peering down at us. Already it was gone from sight again. But the silver bird returned one more time, flew a round at even greater height, and then disappeared into the northeastern sky. None of us still had any thoughts of sleep, cold or hunger. We looked at each other. Many of us were so overcome with profound, excited emotions that we trembled with the effort to control ourselves. But courage and hope now shone from everyone's eyes. –

Now we spent more hours standing lined up. The guards ran busily up and down, divided us into groups, officers appeared and yelled orders, and eventually it was noon. We had been on our feet since five o'clock in the morning and still there was no sign that our march-off would begin. That there would be a march for us had become clear from the guards' conversations.

We were moved back and forth and reassigned over and over again, but finally we were all divided into four big groups of eight hundred to one thousand prisoners each. A tall, slim officer appeared on the scene. He had a yellowish-pale face framed by dark hair. He was very elegantly dressed and went from one group to the next, silently but firm of step, and addressed each group. Having reached our group, he planted himself wide-legged some ten meters ahead of the first row and declared, in a shrill command voice and with arms akimbo, that we would now march off. He expected strict discipline. The guards, he said, had orders to shoot anyone who left his row without permission. And indeed they would act on these orders.

After this address, which was cold and matter-of-fact despite the hateful undertone of his voice, he went on to the next group. The guards assigned to our group approached and almost all of them threatened that "they would show us good" if we did not do as we were told. The sergeants placed the guards in such a way that they would accompany our marching columns at equal intervals to either side of our rows. But for the moment we still stood lined up in rows of four, myself in the last row, my back to the sugar warehouse but some distance from it.

I felt a light touch at my elbow and looked sideways at Mutschler, who stood beside me. He rolled his eyes at me, silently gesturing behind us. I cautiously turned my head a little more and saw how two guards led old man Diesing past behind us. They had taken hold of the old gentleman by either arm, and in this way he shuffled painfully past. His gray hair stuck out tousled from his head; some straw was in it; his face was haggard beyond words, his chin and cheeks covered in thick white stubble. He looked at the ground before him, holding his old gray felt hat in one hand. I turned my head farther right and gazed after him. Two more guards were walking behind him.

"So it's true," I thought, "they really are going to load the oldest ones onto carts." A rumor had spread through our ranks some two hours ago that old and sick prisoners could report to the main gate; carts stood ready for them there.

Ahead and to the right of me stood old man Stübner. I

tugged at his sleeve. "Stübner, don't you want to report as well?" He looked back at me, understanding my intent. But his face was pale and he stared at me in anxious agitation. "Why are four guards going with him? And all of them with guns!" he whispered back.

A horrible suspicion hit me, and suddenly I had to choke back vomit. I looked back again at old Diesing. He was just then stumbling with difficulty around the edge of the warehouse. All comrades to the right of me were looking over their right shoulder, all were listening for a sound from the back. Our ranks were silent. Ahead of us, the guards were talking, and the square itself was as noisy as ever. Talking was not forbidden.

I saw how some comrades ahead of me flinched a little; I too seemed to have heard a frightened, muffled cry. Then two shots rang out in quick succession. I saw two guards behind us run to the edge of the building, and now we clearly heard another single shot. "Those pigs, those damned pigs! An old man, a seventy-year-old man!" Mutschler ground out beside me. "Hush!" Udo Roth whispered sharply. We fell silent. Behind us, the four murderers returned. They did not speak, and returned to their places. I looked after them. One of them busied himself with the lock of his rifle.

Of the three or four thousand Germans standing here in the factory yard, only forty or fifty of us had noticed what had happened. But what was going on in the other groups?

After another hour – it was about one-thirty in the afternoon – we saw the first division march off. Now a Polish lieutenant appeared. He called a few guards over – the sergeants, apparently – and gave them orders. We were to do a right turn. Twenty minutes later we began to move. I hoped to take a glimpse behind the warehouse corner, where old man Diesing's body lay, but the first of us had to turn left again right away. We marched out of the yard. A column of some two hundred men were already waiting on the road, and we had to join up with them. At the very front I saw some women, perhaps sixty in number. So they were to march with us.

Finally, after yet more waiting, the march began. We had had nothing to eat or drink that day, nor the day before. As we had stood lined up since the early morning we also had not had an opportunity to buy any rations again via the women. Even at the very start of our forced march we were weak, tired and listless.

Now we were back on the wide main road on which the panje carts had brought us from Wloclawek two days earlier. It ran along the entire length of the factory grounds and then continued straight as an arrow to the southwest.

It was very hot and there was not a cloud in the sky. We trotted along the sandy street in a cloud of dust raised by thousands of tired feet, floating over and amongst our rows. There was not even a breath of wind. At some distance from either side of the road stood autumn-tinted poplars, rustling golden columns flanking our march. The road ran up a small ridge lying at a right angle to our direction; in the uniformly flat land covered with vast green fields of sugar beets, it seemed like a great height. At the top I looked back. An endless black trail of people extended behind me past the horizon, over which the tall smokestack of the sugar factory reached into the sky.

After some time we reached the town of Chodecz. Our lieutenant called a halt on the market square. To our surprise, the inhabitants kept calm. A lemonade cart was called over; whoever had money could buy a bottle of lemonade. Jews, who had already done their business with the first group ahead of us, approached. "Want to buy apples? Or eggs? Or water?" So here too, the prospect of profit conquered all the hatred they felt for us Nazis. They brought fruit, sour pickles, water. Men and especially women brought water in big buckets. An old peasant woman brought me a big bowl of wonderfully refreshing buttermilk. She watched me with kind eyes as I drank, and when I asked her about the price she said, in Polish and after a quick glance around, that she was a German, that there were many Germans here in Chodecz, and then she hurried off to fetch more refreshments. I ate and drank indiscriminately all I was given. My body craved sustenance and beyond the buttermilk I stuffed myself with three sour pickles, soda water, apples and pears, and topped it off with water. It was not until I was relatively full that I began to consider the consequences of such a food combination. But nothing happened! Our parched organs took and digested everything they were given without rebelling. Later I learned that many Protestant Germans lived in this remote town in the middle of former Russian Poland. Their pastor had not been arrested and carried off, and was able to do many good deeds for his ethnic German brethren passing through Chodecz.

We had been permitted to sit down on the cobblestones, and since everyone who had neither money nor the good fortune to find a German beneficiary was given a share by his neighbors, we resumed our march with our strength somewhat restored.

After a seemingly endless march we came to a small stand of trees. In a grassy vale to the right behind them, two small blue ponds shone under the clear autumn sky. The Polish lieutenant called a halt. For the first and only time on our journey through Poland I suddenly felt all my strength draining from my body. I had an insane urge to step out of our column, and only my sudden weakness prevented me. Slowly, sentences formed in my aching head. "No-one can stop me from going down to that water and lying down in the grass. It's my right. I haven't done anything wrong. I'm a free man. What right do the Poles have to give me orders! I want to bathe now, my feet are sore and dirty, I want to wash them. That's my right, my perfectly good right." Thoughts like that floated foggily through my brain. They were interrupted by a hard grip on my upper arm and the sight of a pair of calm blue eyes in a face of composed resolve. Had I spoken aloud? I thought I heard my name. "It's okay, Reinhold, we'll do all that later when we come back." Had someone said that to me? Lemke? Or Udo Roth? It seems I said it to myself, and woke up.

A few women walked off into the stand of trees. "What are they doing?" I softly asked my neighbor.

"Decent of the lieutenant to allow the women to go into the bushes!" I heard someone say. Yes, that's how far we had come, that we regarded this basic bit of human consideration as chivalry! We men had to answer our calls of nature in the open field to the left of the road.

I was fully awake again. I saw an old woman, white-haired, hunch-backed and lame on one foot, hobbling into the bushes. I had already noticed her in Hohensalza. She too had been deemed so dangerous to the Polish state that they had arrested her and now dragged her along with us here on this odyssey. Another old woman, tall and of large stature, was being led by two young girls wearing thin silk summer stockings and high-heeled sandals. I saw a peasant woman in wooden shoes, carrying an infant in her arms. How was the woman's parched body to make food for the child?! She spent these days watching the precious life in her arms slowly starve to death.

In Chodecz our guards had shown signs of human compassion; they were themselves hungry and thirsty, and it seemed to have produced something like a sense of solidarity with us. Now the reaction set in. Clearly they were ashamed of their earlier weakness. When our columns moved on again, they began to urge us to speed. It was still very hot and we dragged ourselves painfully through the sand. Some carried suitcases that the women had abandoned. In the town, Lemke had bought a pail in which he carried some biscuits and fruit with which to revive anyone who collapsed. The guards prodded and scolded; we were walking too slowly for them.

We turned off the cobblestones onto a broad country road. A red brick church stood to the left of the road. A few poplars, a few willows and birch trees. Sugar beet fields to the left and right, flat, monotonous. Above us, the sun. The dust settled on our lips, in our hair; the road was worn with deep ruts. The sand crept into our shoes. Some farmers wearing slippers, just as they had been dragged from their homes, carried them in their hands and walked in socks or barefoot. Time and again, someone else took off their shoes. The small boost which our rest in Chodecz had given us was long used up.

Every now and then, Polish farmers stood by the side of the road, cursing and threatening. One old hag worked herself up into such a rage that she turned around, lifted her skirts and showed us her naked behind. Mutschler grumbled softly: "If only she were young!" The guards mocked the enraged old woman, she let loose with a string of invective, picked up a rock and threw it at our marching column. It missed.

There was the sound of yelling from ahead. The guards asked what was up. Then they called: "Everyone to the right shoulder!" We were just walking down a slight incline towards a stand of alder trees; dusk was approaching. Dark water shone among thick grass. At the left shoulder of the road a man lay, curled up, face pressed into the sand, his hat beside him in the grass, his full head of white hair discolored red with running blood. His breath rattled. His arms were spread wide, as though in dying he wished to press the earth close to him. The guards drove us over to the right side of the road – we were not supposed to see this. But they were so eager to feast themselves on the sight that they failed to pay enough attention to us.

At the top of the incline behind the stand of alder trees, a younger man some few rows ahead of me stepped briefly out of his marching row and bent down to retie his shoe laces. A guard walked up and shoved him from behind into the ditch; the comrade fell, and before he could even get up the guard had pressed the muzzle of his rifle against his temple and pulled the trigger. It was late afternoon, dusk was approaching, but it was still daylight, still easy to see by. A German human being had simply tried to re-tie his shoes.

From a farmhouse a woman came running over the field. She was still young, she ran quickly. We saw her skirt flapping as she ran. In her hand she carried a pail. We watched her come closer. She was bringing water – filled with pity for us, she wanted to help us. A guard took the pail, which could have refreshed fifty of us, cursed the woman rudely, and dumped the water out onto the ground. The woman stood as if frozen, looked at the man, slowly took up the empty bucket, suddenly tears poured from her eyes, she turned away sobbing and covered her eyes with both hands. And thus she went back to the farmhouse.

A town appeared ahead of us. The first column that was marching the same way ahead of ours had tipped the inhabitants off. The guards had told them who and what we were.

Again there were the curses, threatening fists, distorted enraged faces. Many spat at us. On the market square, which we had to cross diagonally, they came at us with sticks and fence slats. Children and girls threw rocks.

Walking ahead of me was Rosenstiel, tall and blond. "He's fattened himself on Polish sausage, on our bacon, on our bread!" He received punches and kicks, but he continued to look straight ahead. With his left hand he still held his young charge, fourteen-year-old Hans Beierling from Thorn. "Look straight ahead, don't look at anyone!" said Walter Lemke beside me. I was glad that I was not wearing glasses. The march through the town seemed endless.

"Give them to us! Why are you guarding them? We'll rip their guts out!" It was always the same. The Beast in the guise of man.

We looked straight ahead. Just show no fear! But most of us were not afraid. We had become indifferent. Only the slander! – That ate at our pride.

Now it was dark. We had left the town behind us. We had been on our feet since five o'clock in the morning, with two brief breaks. The marching column was silent. We were no soldiers. Even for soldiers it would have been hard, without water, without food. But we were fifty years old and older, with heart conditions, old men, people who were lame or had been beaten until we were lame, we wore light shoes and thin stockings, some walked barefoot, one in slippers. And the women up ahead – they shared in all of it. They were cursed and slandered and vilely insulted, and the guards had been given good advice: "Take that one for the night, she's still young, she's still well padded up front..." That was the least of what they had to hear. Young fellows had walked alongside them, had discussed their various merits, pointed at them, elaborated to each other, drooling, what they would do to them... At least now it was dark, now the women could cry, no-one saw their tears.

We linked arms. Just don't give in. Each dragged the other along, many clenched their teeth, we still managed. There was a palpable sense of pride, of much patience and courage.

But how slowly the journey went on! The dragging of feet across the sand, a bucket rattled, somewhere someone sighed, and how large and bright the stars were, so much more than usual!

Some of the old policemen had been relieved. Now our guards were younger fellows, seventeen-year-olds, so-called *Strzelec,* members of paramilitary Riflemen's Associations. They were fresh and well-rested, they threatened and yelled. *"Marszerowac! Marszerowac!"* Shots rang out every now and then near the end of the column.

A tree grew out of the darkness by the side of the road; we approached it, agonizingly slowly, passed it, left it behind us. To the right, a railroad track parallelled the road, a narrow-gauge track or perhaps a sugar beet spur. Again there was shooting behind us.

Suddenly a voice yelled, right in front of me: "Where is the fellow, where is he?! He wanted to shoot me, he threatened me with his revolver!" It was Rehse, marching just ahead of me. Udo Roth's voice chimed in, calming, soothing; a Strzelec came running, yelling and cursing, fortunately he tripped in the dark and fell. Rehse was quiet again. He had probably been dreaming. All of us were half asleep as we staggered and stumbled along.

"Armistice," came a voice behind me. The word had already come up several times. It became entrenched in our thinking, an *idée fixe,* an obsession. We clung to the belief. Some of us claimed to know that negotiations were underway between Poland and Germany.

I tried to determine our marching direction by the stars

in the sky. The stars were much bigger than normal; it was a long time before I realized that they just seemed so big to me because I was without my glasses. We were marching south, almost southwestwards, I thought. So they're already driving us towards the Silesian border. The word ghosted through our column – "armistice" – everyone hoped. Even the groans of those who could barely go on grew fainter.

On the right, a bright glow came over the fields, it flashed brightly, faded, swept back and forth in big curves. A car was approaching on back roads. Was it coming to tell us that we were to be let go? Already we could make out both headlights, now they vanished again behind some bushes, brightened again, went out. We waited; we stumbled on, but we all looked across the field to our right. It remained dark. No light appeared. It remained dark.

Our guards yelled, driving us onward, faster, faster. We dragged ourselves on. Armistice?

To the left of the road, a low garden wall, and rustling treetops above it. We felt the silent peace under the night-darkened park trees. It was a large estate, a manor house. We thought of quiet rooms, of garden paths, of water, sleep. We staggered down the street. The wall seemed never-ending. We stumbled and faltered past. Thirst. Such thirst. Our tongues were gummy, swollen, the dust sat on our lips, in our throats, our lungs.

Suddenly, unrest up ahead. We don't want to hear it. The trees rustle – so soothing. But now the wall has ended. A flashlight blinds us, shines on us, and another one. Lemke, suddenly wide awake, whispers: "Look, there are artillery guns over there!" We listen to a conversation between our guards and a few soldiers. Yes, that's an artillery gun; this is the outpost of an artillery regiment.

We are half asleep and don't understand right away what it means that this is an artillery position. But then someone says it, softly: "we're in the battle zone." They're close, close, they'll catch up to us. No-one says it out loud but everyone thinks it: "they" – that's our soldiers, the German soldiers. We have no other word for them; we need no other word.

After we have left the manor house behind, we see the glow of fire, far off to the left. Houses are burning there! A town is on fire. There's fighting over there. They're close. Some cries come from among our ranks. Whispering. We move closer together, even though our feet ache and burn we tighten our ranks. A shot is fired behind us, another follows right away. One of the *Strzelec* yells angrily, more and more shots are fired, but it's far back, it's not in our group any more.

Now we also hear a low growling sound, every now and then – it's not frequent, but when it comes the air rumbles and rolls in waves across the open countryside. Artillery fire. Off to the right, to the southwest, we also see the glow of fire now. And from over there as well, we hear the snarling angry rumble, and time and again there is a quickly-fading glow in the sky, like a bright fan opening and closing.

We pass through another town. It's the heart of night, no-one is in the streets. The uneven cobblestones are agony to our worn-down feet. My chafed toes burn like fire, but the Germans are close, our soldiers are close. The Poles are nervous, especially the young ones, you can hear it. Up ahead

I hear voices, I can't make out much but I hear threats. Then everyone dozes off again.

Behind the town – it was Krosniewice – we get to rest. We sit down in the ditches, in the damp grass. One asks for water. "Over there," a guard replies. The comrade stands up, looks in the direction indicated. "Is it true? We'll get water there?" "Yes, the lieutenant said so," answers the guard. "It's not far to where the fire is," our comrade tells us, "it's very bright." Now we can see the fire too, we have all stood up to look. It's a red glow on the horizon. But then we sit down again, silent. It was the moon, just rising, glowing like a fire on the horizon. Yes, on the moon, no doubt we'll get water there.

"Behold how the moon rises over the sleeping world," a fervent voice suddenly said from among our ranks, some ten or twelve rows back. "It rises thus over the world every night. And the stars are in the sky and shine down on us as they have done for time immemorial. Trust in the stars, dear brothers, one day we too shall enjoy the peace of eternity..."

There was astonished silence all around. A preacher was speaking. I felt nervous anger rising inside myself. But already a hard voice said from out of the dark: "Someone shut that ass up!" The preacher fell silent.

Three figures, Poles, came down the long row of resting prisoners, searching. They called a name, a guard answered. They went to him. "Where is he? Where?" a horrible voice asked. "That's him, over there!"

"Well, now we've got you, now we'll show you!" one of the Poles screamed in hysterical rage. He must have had some old grudge. We heard a cry, and a dull blow as though a hard object had impacted a human body. A policeman jumped up, screamed at us: "Everyone lie down! You will lie down! Anyone raising his head will be shot!" They surrounded us in the darkness, rifles at the ready, and we could not move... but from up ahead we heard shrieks, a German comrade was screaming, and in between, the words of the Poles, over and over again: "There, take that! And that! And that!" We heard the blows rain down on the victim's body.

Our comrade was reduced to whimpers: "Shoot me dead, why don't you, I was a soldier, shoot me, don't beat me to death like this."

We lay there in the night, in the dark, the stars were high in the sky, the narrow sickle of the moon, I lay facing upwards, on the edge of the ditch, and heard the dull pounding of cudgels and truncheons on the body and arms of a fellow human being, a comrade. It all happened barely ten meters from me. Now they were dragging him off across the field. My ears picked it all up – the sound of the body bumping across the field, through the sugar beets.

"Here's some brush, we'll finish him off here!" they said, out of breath from all their hard work. We heard every word, it clawed into our hearts, all of it, every groan, every whimper and scream and the sound of every punch and blow. And now they were kicking and trampling him.

The stars shone, and the moon; the night breeze wafted across the field. When the order came, we lined up and stumbled on.

After two minutes' marching we had forgotten the

incident. My feet burned like fire. I had cut the back of my right shoe open with a knife. It helped a little.

A train rolled up beside and past us on the tracks of the narrow-gauge spur. We had to stop while it crossed the road before us. We leaned against each other and slept. We tottered back and forth, some talked in their sleep, groaned, sighed. I did not sleep. My eyes burned with exhaustion. Lemke too, standing to my left, was awake. Those most exhausted propped themselves on those still awake, on all sides; thus we stood supported by those at the end of their strength; their breath was ours, and we held them up. Up in the sky the moon shone yellow. A bat flitted back and forth above us. Then we began to move again, the way was clear, staggering we walked on. *"Marszerowac! Marszerowac!"* the guards roared.

Yelling voices carried over to us from one side. The sound of driving cars and carts grew louder by the minute. The crack of whips, human voices, curses, sobbing. We were approaching a major road. On it, a hunted people were fleeing. It was the paved main road from Posen to Warsaw. We pushed our way into the rushing stream. What was going on around us wasn't that important, far more important was that the smooth concrete road was easier on our feet. This was no bumpy cobblestone, no rutted back road with potholes and cart tracks. We no longer needed to lift our feet, we only had to slide them ahead, dragging across the ground. For many, it was what saved them at the last moment.

Cars drove with dimmed or no lights; city carriages piled high with bedding, with boxes, with furniture and baskets under which the people were barely visible; panje carts on which women sat and children slept; bicyclists; pedestrians pushing wheel barrows or baby carriages overloaded with luggage. Infantry columns came towards us, munitions transports, supply cars, horse-drawn, and then the stream of refugees spread out again to take up the entire road. Many of them yelled at us, every now and then we heard a cry of pain, but most of them were too tired, too weary. Those sitting in the cars slept or stared at nothing. Women wept. We were pushed onward.

Ahead of us the sky grew lighter. Dawn approached. Fog rose from the fields. We slept while walking, kept our arms linked left and right, we were tired, so tired. One supported the other. Stübner was seventy-two years old, Heinecke over sixty and with a heart condition, Lehmann-Nitsche over sixty and lame on one leg, Naue still suffered the effects of a head injury a Pole had caused him two years earlier with a fence slat, Milbradt had rheumatism and could barely still hobble along. All of them were held up and supported by the rest of us who were younger, stronger, healthier. None from our group was to be left behind. For we heard the cries from the back of the column, we heard the gunshots and the cursing of the guards; and we knew what it meant. It galvanized us time and again, no, leave no-one behind, no-one. Rehse moaned pitifully to himself; he believed the Poles had it in for him in particular and were coming to get him. "Hide me!" he begged, sobbing, "hide me, don't give me away!" He was already half out of his mind that night.

In the dawn, the hay ricks to the left and right of the road looked like dark mountains.

We crossed railroad tracks. Mills stood to the right. A train station, walls blackened by fire, no roofs left on the buildings, no windows left in the walls, clouds of smoke. A track, a thick iron track, reached up into the sky bent grotesquely into a half-circle. Beside it, a large crater. An iron wheel lay at its bottom. We staggered past.

A town appeared from out of the fog ahead of us. Clouds of smoke drifted over it. We stopped again. There was a head count. We were given some bread, one loaf per sixteen men. The morning cold had awakened us. We were not allowed to have knives, they had been taken from us, but some of us had one anyway. Udo Roth divided our loaf into sixteen equal pieces but no-one could eat his portion. Our mouths could not produce saliva, tongues, lips, throats were parched powder-dry. "Put it in your pockets, we'll get water somewhere and then we can eat it," said Lemke. His pail was empty; he had distributed all his remaining fruit and biscuits during this night's march.

We tottered on, into the town that still lay sleeping, and had to sit down in the market square. We looked around us. Many houses had been knocked down, others were still standing. Somebody said that this was Kutno.

It grew light. The first inhabitants of the town appeared in the basement or main doors or at the windows. And now the howling roar descended on us again; in just a few minutes the square was filled to bursting, always the same curse words, the same threats, the same gestures. Jews, most were Jews. Our heads dropped onto our knees and we slept amidst the raging, roiling fury.

After just an hour, the order came to march on, eastward. The rest had given us new strength, but still, when we were to get up it was like walking over red-hot iron. The first few steps were almost more than we could take. But the guards used cudgels and sticks, we had to help comrades even weaker than ourselves, had to pull them up, support them, drag them on – talk sense kindly or even harshly to those who wanted to be left behind – it helped us get through the first few minutes.

Outside Kutno, a man ten rows ahead of us staggered out of line and fell into the ditch, into the grass. A *Strzelec* lost his patience, ran over, screamed vile curses, pressed the muzzle of his carbine to the man's head and fired. Without a sound our comrade rolled the rest of the way into the ditch, his face staring upward. The shooter, a young person no older than sixteen, stood beside him as if turned to stone. Suddenly he began to shriek horribly. "I shot him, my God, my God, I shot him, I'm a murderer, Mother of God help me, I shot him!" He staggered away across the field, took a few steps, his voice cracked, he collapsed among the sugar beets, his screams grew duller: "I murdered him, an innocent man, murdered a human being, *matka boska, matka boska...*"

Other guards ran over and sought to calm the screamer; we marched on, past our comrade's lifeless body. His head lay in a pool of blood. He was wearing a colorful shirt – it was checked green and white – a pair of torn pants, and gray stockings but no shoes. His left hand was cramped around a small bundle of his possessions.

Suddenly a man ran away across the margin of a field. I had not seen him leave our column, I only noticed him when the guards began to shout. They knelt down and shot after the fleeing man. It was senseless to try to escape now – it was broad daylight. He had either wanted to die, or had lost his grip on sanity. A bullet hit him – or was he trying to fool the guards? He fell into a depression in the ground. Two Poles ran over. Two, three, four shots from their carbines. They came slowly back. These two did not shriek in mortification because they had murdered a human being.

"Look up!" a German voice said behind me, not too loudly. "Look up, comrades, above us, look up!" The man barely stifled a sob, but we could hear that it was a sob of joy. Our senses were strangely heightened during these days.

We looked up into the morning sky, we heard the hum above us that became a drone. A German plane raced over us, from the front of the column, the machine was sideways in the air, they looked down on us from their seats up there, they raced along the entire road, along the entire immense length of our column. They had to, yes, they **had** to see what we were, they had to see the bayonets, the guards on either side of our lines, and also that we ourselves were unarmed. Columns of fleeing Poles looked different, they included panje carts, cars, trucks, they were disorganized, milling, screaming masses. We on the other hand, we walked in strict rows of four. They had to have recognized us. Get help! Tell our people behind the frontlines what you saw, fetch them here, tell them to hurry, three thousand Germans are being hounded to death here, beaten, shot by the wayside, hurry...!

None of us spoke a word, no cry tore free, no-one waved. Only our eyes followed his flight path.

There he was again, much higher this time. He flew large circles above us, over and over, he rose higher and higher. From up there he had to be able to see the entire length of our marching column.

Then suddenly he vanished into the blue of the sky. We did not see or hear him again.

"He's gone to report where we are," said someone's voice. Not loudly, but firmly. Had it been me? Or Walter Lemke? Or old man Stübner, who was an ever-unbroken spirit even though his old body was on the verge of collapse? It didn't matter. Everyone thought it: "He's gone to report what he saw here."

It grew hot again. But the visit from the German plane had given us strength. We marched on, and marched on, and on and on and on.

8

The Last Day and the Last Night

A large estate to the left of the road, looming red buildings, long livestock stables, barns, sheds. We saw the vanguard of our column turn off into the yard. We trotted through the gate. To the left behind it stood a hollowed-out tree trunk that served as water trough for livestock. It was crowded round by pushing, shoving, yelling people dying of thirst. The guards herded us on. "You'll get water on the meadow!" they said.

We staggered more than walked across the yard, out another gate, along a brick wall. The first group from our column was already lying on the meadow in the grass. We were assigned a spot beside them, and collapsed to the ground.

The place was without shade and the sun broiled down mercilessly, but we were allowed to rest. Our hearts pounded in our chests, still doing their duty. Our feet burned. We must have lain as though lifeless for half an hour. Then young Meister came up with a bucket of water. It was distributed among our group; we drank the bucket empty, not a drop was left. Meister returned to the yard, he took the young girl along who had obtained bread for us on the sugar factory yard, and he fetched water for the women. Even these guards were more amenable if there was a woman along.

Meister repeated his trip numerous more times. He had to put up with curse words, threats, punches, but he did not give up, and other younger comrades joined him in bringing water. Later, a cart with a water barrel came by, all of us received a little water, some even got enough.

We had been on our feet since early morning of the day before. We had stood in the yard of the sugar factory from six o'clock until two in the afternoon, the march-off had begun at about three. For the entire afternoon, the entire endlessly long night, and throughout the morning hours we had marched, with perhaps two or three rest breaks of any note. Yesterday evening we had received a slice of bread, that was all. During the night, if ever we had been allowed to sit briefly at the side of the road, we had dug turnips and even potatoes out of the ground with our bare fingers, and eaten those to try to quench our thirst at least a little.

We had barely a glance for the two groups arriving after us. They staggered up tired, ragged, weaving on their feet, with gray faces, covered in dust, dull-eyed, and threw themselves down on the grass as we had done.

Names of comrades who had been shot or beaten to death were passed around: Albert Schröder from Deutsch-Westfalen, Robert Bitzer from Gross-Lonk, Franz Pankalla, Hugo Zühlke from Netzwalde, a fifteen-year-old... I remember only a very few of them. But I saw that Senator Busse still lived, and others whom I had given up for dead stumbled up to us, supported by their neighbors, or even being carried the last few steps. How much silent, matter-of-fact self-sacrifice, how much eager willingness to help, how much tough endurance everywhere!

A few carts with the weak, the sick, the most elderly arrived. We had to lift them from their places, lay them in the grass, moisten their brows, their hands. Ortwig, whom I met again here, told me in a whisper that there was a cart in the manor yard with ten or twelve dead comrades on it. "Are they really dead, or just so exhausted that they couldn't move any longer?" "No, they're stacked on top of each other, their feet are hanging down over the end. They're dead," he replied, in a voice made terrible by its lifeless, choked monotone.

At the edge of the meadow lay a small swampy pool. I saw that comrades were washing themselves there, faltered over there as well, took off my shoes and socks, put my feet into the water, rubbed the coating of filth off my soles and heels, picked some green leaves, wrapped them around my toes and heels, pulled my socks back over it all. Now it was bearable to stand up again. I returned to my place, almost cheerful. On my way I was stopped. Editor Kuss, whose apartment in Hohensalza had been in the same building as mine, offered me a cigarette. I took it, smoked a few puffs; I felt as though I had just had a refreshing breakfast. Others finished the cigarette.

Despite the heat I slept a little. In the afternoon we had to line up again. Our journey went on.

When we walked out onto the road – it was still the

wide concrete road leading to Warsaw – we were sucked into the stream of refugees again. An entire nation fled eastward. Women in cars, in elegant clothes, made up and with painted lips; peasants in well-worn work clothes walked beside small panje carts in which children sat on bedding and boxes, pigs squealed under bales piled high, bare-footed boys herded a goat or a cow, chickens clucked, dogs barked, a private car or rented carriage from Posen pushed through the milling crowds honking its horn. A horse-drawn medical corps rattled past us and we saw the German apothecary from Mogilno, whom we all knew, sitting on the box seat wearing a Polish uniform. None of us called to him, none of us wanted to give him away; he stared down at us, he knew that we were Germans but probably didn't recognize any of us in our present state.

A unit of Polish troops passed us, heading westward. They had no rifles or bayonets. Were the Poles so short of weapons, or did they not trust their own soldiers? The officer leading the first company coming towards us kept his men together and forbade them any maltreatment, but the very next company beat down on us with spades and cudgels that some of the men picked up from the side of the road.

"How much longer is this going to go on? How much longer do they plan to keep doing this to us?" Lehmann-Nitsche suddenly asked in despair. He was lame on one leg, and it had taken him superhuman strength to keep up his courage to this point. Lemke patted him on the shoulder, indestructible, Lemke was the soul and pillar of our group, he said: "No more than another forty-eight hours, my word on it, no longer. Look at them – look how they're fleeing. Our boys are hard on their heels, and they'll catch up to us."

The more dusk settled over the countryside, the more people streamed onto the road from out of the surrounding woods and bushes. During the day many kept themselves hidden out of fear of the German planes; in the evening they dared come out.

We were exhausted to death, our bodies pumped dry, the great heat of that afternoon had not wrung one drop of sweat out of us, our tongues were parched, we staggered, limped, crept forward. And yet, we left no-one behind. The older ones among us began to fail; we dragged them along, supported them under their arms. Just don't drop back, just don't fall by the roadside. Gunshots sounded behind us and we all knew what it meant. And so we shuffled into the evening, spat at, cursed at, stones thrown at us; we kept our eyes ahead, said not a word, held each other up by our arms, and marched.

Behind us rumbled the sounds of battle. The Germans were coming, the German artillery pounded the ground behind us with iron fists. Towards evening the rumble grew louder, they were coming closer. Smoke from burning villages wafted across the fields. Already we could make out individual detonations. When it was dark we counted the seconds between the flash of the fire and the roar of the shot. We got to twenty-six. So they were only nine kilometers behind us. On all sides to the south, west and north, fires could be seen burning, the sounds of war roared and pounded and rumbled at us from everywhere; we were encircled, and the only escape from the cauldron was to the east.

Wild rumors abounded. The Poles yelled details to each other, we listened greedily and believed nothing we heard. The stars shone above us in a clear sky but we did not look up. We looked straight ahead, our ears strained backwards, the essence of our selves listened. Were they closer?

That night Rehse lost his mind. He tried to break rank, we held on to him, had to fight with him. I kept him in line for perhaps an hour, held his arm in an iron grip, encouraged and cajoled him, and forced him on with punches if necessary whenever he tried to stop. He sobbed, begged, tried to throw himself on the ground, tried to flee, I clung to him like a snarling dog. Later, Udo Roth took over. We got Rehse through.

Shots from the guards' rifles cracked ahead of us, behind us. Those who were beaten down or stabbed barely even screamed any more, we heard them groan or whimper at best. One went stark raving mad, leaped at one of the guards. It was just a brief struggle.

A village appeared before us, a church steeple towered tall and black. Beside the church, artillery was firing incessantly. We lay in the roadside ditch, a water's surface glittered to the left of the street, reflecting the moon, tall trees rustled loudly. Someone brought water in a bucket, we crowded round him, everyone got a mouthful, it tasted of sewage but everyone drank, greedily, blissfully, gratefully.

"The march ends in Lowicz, we'll be put on a train in Lowicz!" Nobody knew who'd said it. The rumor skipped through our rows. Many welcomed the thought of being loaded up – it meant an end to our marching. But we said: "Walk more slowly. They'll catch up to us. Once we're on the train we're all lost." In this way our will to resist reasserted itself time and again. Every marching group had men like Walter Lemke, Udo Roth, Stübner, they were hard, tough, fearless. We walked even more slowly. Even our guards were trying not to stagger. And they had received rations, food and all the water they wanted!

The moon shone, it seemed to have grown a bit brighter. The hubbub of the fleeing nation around us had quieted – everyone was tired.

A column of uniformed soldiers passed us, marching in lockstep. They did not beat at us, did not curse us, they were silent. Then, a soft grim voice: "Hold on! They're almost here!" That had been said in German. Now we saw that these soldiers were under guard by others. They were ethnic Germans who had been forced into the Polish army. The Poles did not trust them, had disarmed them, sent them to the rear. A miracle that they hadn't been shot yet.

And the artillery fire roared behind us. We limped, crept on even more slowly.

A bridge over a wide stream crosses our road. It's already dawn. A prisoner drops over the stone parapet into the shallow water below, the guards fire, he's standing up to his knees in the water, bends down, fills his hat with water, drinks and drinks. The bullets splash into the stream beside him, he drinks and drinks, dips his hat full once more, wades to the shore, runs up the embankment, rejoins his marching column, he has not been hit. The guard in charge of his group silently lets him back in, he's one of the few who do not participate in the slaughter. The dripping hat is handed from one to the next, everyone takes a few sips and passes it on; ten, twelve people are a little less parched than before.

There's a brackish water hole by the roadside. Some try to run to it, to fetch water. The Poles drive them back with blows from their rifle butts. One comrade begs for water; a guard takes the man's canteen, walks to the water hole, fills the canteen, brings it back, two trembling hands reach for it, ten, twenty pairs of eyes are fixed on the bulging bottle, the Pole turns it upside down, pours its contents on the ground, walks along beside the column, holds the bottle out before himself as he walks, the water gurgles out and disappears into the sand.

Two men from the last group who could no longer take the thirst ran out of their row at this same water hole. They ran the few steps, they had no containers, they knelt down, scooped the brown liquid with their hands. Two Poles walked across the grass, seized them by their heels from behind, tipped the two drinkers into the water, held them by their feet until they no longer moved. Then they let them go. "Now they've got enough water in their guts," said one of the murderers.

A railroad track came over from the right, then another one, then more and more converged. We were approaching the train station. From out of the fog, a town appeared, covered by a dense layer of smoke. Occasional tongues of flame licked upwards. It was light now, bright morning, veiled over by drifting banks of smoke and fog. The past night was an ugly dream. Soldiers had thrown hand grenades among us, had beaten us with spades, white-haired men lay murdered on the ground. Now we saw the women again, walking ahead of us. Indeed, they had survived it all too. Now it was light, the cool dawn air was refreshing.

Suddenly, beside me, Lemke bent down. He had received just as little water as the rest of us, and had eaten no more than anyone else. Where did he find the strength? He picked something up off the ground, a shiny object, held it up, showed it around! "Today we'll get something to eat, comrades. Look, I've already found the spoon!" How good such words did us all.

We were herded off the road down onto a narrow path. Ahead of us lay the burning city, a long row of small square wooden houses stood to our left, and behind them, a large flat meadow, with a small stand of pines at its far edge. We walked along it. The artillery had been silent for hours.

Suddenly there was a crash ahead of us, toxic clouds of smoke plumed up from the earth and there were ear-splitting explosions. The air above us howled. We threw ourselves into the roadside ditch. An iron fence stood there, and big red buildings on a large yard. The guards yelled and screamed: "Up! Back! Everyone on the meadow!"

"Keep off the road, get away from the tracks here!" I heard Walter Lemke say. His voice was completely changed: hard and quick. I looked at him, his lips were clenched, face dark as a thundercloud. "Man, Reinhold!" he said. We hurried, stooping, along the ditch, urging the others along.

"To the right, onto the meadow!" Udo Roth was now also yelling, "away from the tracks!" What were they so upset about? His voice carried sharply, as though he were an officer again, instructing his unit. Again there was a howling whistle above us, then an infernal crash, we ran, hundreds ran. Where were our guards? I saw none. They were gone, had run away.

"Not that far, not that far!" I heard someone roar. A rattling sound filled the air, and I threw myself into a dry ditch that zig-zagged through the meadow. "Trenches?" I thought. "Here?" They had been very hastily dug. The machine gun still rattled. We huddled behind the trench walls. We looked into each other's flickering eyes and saw hope. Great God, could it be true?

A piercing cry: "A plane! A plane!" We looked up, from the sky a gleaming silver bird rushed down, it circled over us, we could not lift our heads above the trenches for the machine gun fired its rounds right over the grass. Now another voice rang out: "He's putting a red flag out!" And another: "He sees us, he sees us!" Just a few seconds, and then it rushed, howled, hissed above us again, and then there were detonations that made the earth tremble. The sand skittered down our trench walls. And now there was a new rumble in the air, planes high above us, several planes, eight or ten or twelve of them, and now bombs crashed and thundered down from above, they landed distant from us, more towards the Poles. They had arrived – they separated us from the Poles. They had been called in, they had been told about us, our Fatherland had not forgotten us – it struck, now it struck. Grenades and aerial bombs hung a curtain between us and the Poles. We were in the battle zone between the frontlines.

Thus it went on for an hour, eased off a little, returned, for two hours perhaps. Then, suddenly, silence. And then a cry, a shining, bright, clear voice, heightened to superhuman registers by overwhelming joy: "German soldiers! German soldiers at the tracks!"

It catapulted us up. Yelling, running, stumbling, tears, piercing loud cries, the entire field a sea of sobbing, laughing people, rushing forward, we fell, jumped up, ran, the women in our midst, we carried the lame, the sick, the old right along with us, grabbed them under their arms, loud cries like a song, a wave, a crescendo, Heil, Heil, Heil Hitler! Heil Hitler! Our voices failed and yet we shouted, mouths smiling, lips trembling, tears coursing down. Our hearts? Could our hearts bear it – this, too? Could a human heart bear this?

There they stood, our soldiers, ours, just a few, ridiculously few, young, almost children, blond, smiling, under steel helmets, dusty, sweaty, they let us hug them, kiss them, did not fend us off. We stood around, lay on the ground, pounded the earth with legs and fists, shouted, laughed, sobbed.

Until – had much time passed, or just a little? I don't know – until silence fell, and we all stood up and joined in a song. The singing rose and fell; like a wave it ebbed when only a few sang while the others choked back their emotions, and like a wave it soared when everyone had regained control. Arms raised in a holy vow. Germany was among us. –

9

Walter Milbradt Arrives

Later I sat outside a small guard house by the train station. A soldier had given me half a cup of cold coffee and I drank it with slow, very slow sips. I sat on the ground, in the shade, leaning my back against the wall of the building. The other comrades were all camped out beside the Bzura river that ran past near our meadow, they washed up, bathed and rested.

I heard Udo Roth speak. I could see him, he stood on the railway embankment, a little higher than the rest, where everyone could see him. He spoke calmly and strongly of Germany, of the Führer and the new order. Just shortly before, he had been the one to report to a German officer that the Poles had diverted some 600 to 800 comrades farther eastward. "Then I will send some armored cars after them right away!" the German officer had cried – and was gone. Thus it was Udo Roth who had seen to it that the group headed to Bromberg was also liberated that very same day. – Now he stood there on the embankment and spoke to us of the Führer.

But then my gaze was drawn elsewhere. Something was moving, up ahead of me, it was approaching over a swell in the ground and I couldn't quite make out what it was. But now – it was a man – he was closer, he had climbed the small height. And kept coming closer.

God is my witness, I am not lying: a man was coming on his knees. He dragged one knee before the other to move forward. And on his shoulders he carried a comrade. There were only twenty meters now between him and me and the station house. I stared dumbfounded at the approaching man and I was incapable of getting up to help him.

There came my comrade Walter Milbradt from Altreden, who no longer had the strength to walk on his feet, he came on his knees, carrying a man who had lost his life to a Polish machine gun in the very moment of our liberation. He dragged himself right up to where I sat, and gently let the dead man slip to the ground. The German soldier in his steel helmet still stood beside me, and neither of us were able to move as we stared at the scene before us. Walter Milbradt looked at us, his eyes reflecting the dawn of freedom, and collapsed into the grass beside the body of his dead comrade. His strength was exhausted. He passed out.

For more than a kilometer he had carried the dead man, on his knees. He let the others run ahead to the German soldiers, let them rush past him, and carried his burden, did not leave it behind, even though his heart drew him no less fervently than all the others to where they rejoiced and sang the songs of Germany. Any doctor, any athlete, any know-it-all will tell you that such a deed is not possible because it goes beyond human strength. And yet it happened, on September 9, 1939 just outside Lowicz in Poland.

Walter Milbradt was unconscious, his strength had left him, he lay beside his dead comrade. But he would awaken, and then he would be free. –

10

Finis & Credits

And that, my comrades, is how we marched into the Reich, on our long journey through Poland. And like Walter Milbradt, we all come bringing our dead with us on our backs. If anyone should ever undertake to put up a memorial to the Germans in Poland, let it depict a man dragging himself up a hill on his knees and, with a dead man on his shoulders, seeing Freedom.

Our homeland, Posen, bled like no other German border land. Now the Vistula and the Warthe, the Netze and Drewenz and the lakes and cities and towns, the forests and hills and fields of our homeland are German again. The blood of the murdered, the tears of the widows and orphans, the faith of the living have made our land part of the heart of the Reich.

Some are already beginning to disparage what we lived through! And yet – the seeds sown in these weeks of sacrifice will begin to grow. It is enough that we know, and that our children know, what we endured for the sake of Germany.

* * *

This book is based on accounts which were made available to me partly in writing, partly orally in person. My thanks goes to Paul Jendrike from Bromberg, von Rosenstiel from Lipie, Walter Milbradt from Altreden, Peter Schrey from Raschleben, Viktor Ortwig from Kruschwitz, Walter Lemke from Luisenfelde, Julius Mutschler from Ostwehr, Wilhelm Meister, Bruno Schneider, and my brother Reinhold Wittek from Hohensalza. I have also drawn on reports published in the *Deutsche Rundschau* of Bromberg and in the *Posener Tageblatt*. And thanks to Hans Ulrich Hempel I was able, together with my brother and Walter Lemke, to drive by car along the route of this death march and to inspect first-hand the various stations mentioned in these pages.

E. W.

For more books on this subject and many other little-known aspects of German history, please visit us at VersandbuchhandelScriptorium.com and our sister site wintersonnenwende.com !

Featured publications include:

The German original of *Long Night's Journey Into Day:*
• *Der Marsch nach Lowitsch.* Scriptorium, Canada 2023.

• Edwin Erich Dwinger: *Death in Poland. The Fate of the Ethnic Germans in September 1939.* Scriptorium, Canada 2021.
as well as the German original:
• *Der Tod in Polen. Die volksdeutsche Passion.* Eugen Diederichs Verlag, Jena, 1940. Reprinted by The Scriptorium in 2000.

• *The Polish Atrocities Against the German Minority in Poland.* Edited and published by order of the Foreign Office and based upon documentary evidence. Volk und Reich Verlag, Berlin 1940,
as well as the German original:
• *Die polnischen Greueltaten an den Volksdeutschen in Polen.* Im Auftrage des Auswärtigen Amtes auf Grund urkundlichen Beweismaterials zusammengestellt. Volk und Reich Verlag, Berlin 1940.

More titles are being added regularly in German and English.